The Christian Today

by

Jean Daniélou, S.J.

Translated by
Kathryn Sullivan, R.S.C.J.

DESCLEE COMPANY

NEW YORK - TOURNAI - PARIS - ROME 1960

NIHIL OBSTAT
JAMES F. RIGNEY, S. T. D.
Censor Librorum

IMPRIMATUR   January 27, 1960
✠ FRANCIS CARDINAL SPELLMAN
Archbishop of New York

The nihil obstat and imprimatur are official declarations that a book or pamphlet is free of doctrinal or moral error. No implication is contained therein that those who have granted the nihil obstat and imprimatur agree with the contents, opinions or statements expressed.

Library of Congress Catalog Card Number : 60-10016

Printed and bound in Belgium by Desclée & Cie., S. A., Tournai

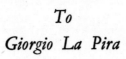

To
Giorgio La Pira

Contents :

Holiness

I

Holiness is God Himself. This is the name which best expresses what He properly is. All His other names : Justice, Love, Truth, are borrowed from the realm of creatures. But when we say that He is holy we mean that He is utterly different from everything we can know, we mean that He is the Totally-Other;[1] and we try to express the intensity of His existence — an intensity so great that man cannot see Him and live. Saint John of the Cross tells us that God is darkness because the dazzling brightness of His light sears our eyes. We recall that when He manifests Himself at times, it is almost more than man can bear, and yet these " showings " through created things are but the borders of His paths, or as it is said in the book of Job, " the fringe of His robe, " so we ask ourselves if we could ever bear the " thunder of His power " (26 : 14).

[1] See van Imschoot, *Théologie de l'Ancien Testament;* Belgium, Desclée & Cie., 1954, I, pp. 42-51.

His holiness, however, is more than the crushing weight of His glory, it is also His supereminent perfection which presses irresistibly upon us and to which we cannot refuse the absolute homage of our admiration and of our love which is called adoration. Here is to be found the basis of all religion, the unconditional acknowledgement of a perfection that is infinite and divine. There can be no doubt that the greatest misery of our age is that this supremely real God is now so absent, that this supremely lovable God is now a subject of such indifference. Today it is the Christian's first duty to rediscover the meaning of God and to bring Him to our age.

However, revelation's proper object is not to teach us that God is holy, but to tell us that through an act of love, as incomprehensible as is this holiness itself, we are called to share in a holiness which is proper to God and which separates Him infinitely from us. In Christ, the divine nature is united with His human nature and sanctifies it by penetrating it with the life of God. Christ is " the Holy One of God, " as we read in the Acts of the Apostles (3 : 14). This He is in His very being, where His humanity is entirely holy because it belongs to the person of the Son of God. This He is in His operations, through the total adhesion, in obedience and love, of His human will to His divine will.

But the Word of God assumed the individual humanity to which it is united only in order to communicate divine life to mankind as a whole. In Him the fire of divine Love was kindled in one point of our nature. But this fire wishes to spread to all mankind, in order that all may be aflame. " I have come to cast fire upon the earth, and what will I but that it be kindled? " (Luke 12 : 49). This fire is holiness. It is communicated by the Holy Spirit. The Holy Spirit is at work in mankind seeking to possess every human soul — and it is at work in the interior of each soul until each soul is completely sanctified. For God must be all in all.

The Holy Spirit acts through the Church. The Church is holy. This is one of its fundamental notes. The Church is holy inasmuch as it is in the Church that holiness is present. Therefore to become a saint it is necessary to enter the Church. This holiness is given at baptism and through this act of incorporation in the Church the Holy Spirit is communicated. In this basic sense, every baptized soul is holy with an objective holiness. Every baptized soul is consecrated to the Trinity. Saint Paul calls the Christians of Corinth " the saints, " οἱ ἅγιοι (1 : 2). Nothing can take away holiness of this kind. A baptized soul can be unfaithful; a baptized soul can never cease to be consecrated.

If holiness is communicated by the sacraments, it is also by the sacraments that holiness grows. Holiness plunges the Christian into Eucharistic life. In Christianity there is no opposition, on the contrary there is rigorous dependence between sacraments and morality, liturgy and prayer. Saint Paul understood the Sunday assembly, where Christ Risen is present in the midst of the community who have come together in His name, to be the place where charisms are communicated. It is in this sense that Christian life is communal because in the community the Holy Ghost is present.

Thus, to be a Christian means to belong to a holy people : " You are, " says the First Epistle of Peter, " a chosen race, a royal priesthood, a holy nation, a purchased people " (2 : 9). Progressively throughout history is this people fashioned. This is true history. This is sacred history. In other words, here in our midst God continues to perform His admirable works, works which are really divine, works which are greater than the great discoveries of learned men, greater than the great exploits of men of action. And these admirable works are the works of holiness, accomplished by the sacraments which are the continuation of the mighty works of God to which the two Testaments testify. These are the realities of the order of charity.

* *

But this is only one aspect. To be a saint is it enough to be baptized, or to receive communion? From our hearts comes the answer, no. From the depths of our hearts come Bloy's words : " There is but one sorrow, that of not being a saint. " For this sorrow we grieve the more deeply because the present drama of the Church is caused by the mediocrity of Christians. As we have just said, when the world looks at Christians it has the right to find in them a reflection,

as it were, of the glory of the Trinity. The world
has a right to discover in their faith, their hope,
their charity a testimony to the presence of the
Holy Spirit, the Spirit of intelligence, of power,
of love. It cannot be denied that often when men
now cast us out, they do so because they deny
Christ; sometimes perhaps it may happen that they
cast us out because they have failed to find in us
Him whom they seek. " I love Christ but I do
not love Christians, " Gandhi used to say.

It is not enough to be baptized. Grace
places in us a principle of sanctity. This principle
must grow. Grace unites us to Christ. This Christ-
life must become ours. We must " be clothed with
Jesus Christ " : " As the One who called you
is holy, be you also holy in all your behavior;
for it is written, ' You shall be holy, because I am
holy ' " (1 Pet. 1 : 15 f). The divine powers which
are in us through baptism must take possession
of us. Claudel says so well that we must evangelize
all the faculties of our soul. We must become saints.

It may be objected, evangelical perfection is a special call. It is too much to ask
that all Christians become saints. It is already
something that they are Christians. To say this
is to err. Every Christian is called to holiness.
Only means vary. The holiness of the layman does
not differ from the holiness of the monk. There
is but one holiness and this holiness is asked of
all men because the Father loves only the Son;
and only those who have clothed themselves with
the Son will enter the Father's house. To be a saint
merely means that the soul is being transformed

in this life. Those who are not saints will experience this transformation in purgatory's purifying fire. Saints undergo this transformation here.

Still, it may further be objected, is there not some pride in this? God does not demand that we be saints but He does ask us to acknowledge that we are sinners. This is a serious question. And this question shows what a low level willed effort, which is the essential aspect of holiness, has reached today. True, the humble avowal of our misery is the whole route. Virtue at this moment has a bad press where its intransigence is easily mocked. Our world, conditioned by psychoanalysis, finds plenty of excuses for sin and sees in it what is ordinary and normal. Willed effort is castigated as a dangerous throw-back. What is even worse : virtue is quickly suspected of pharisaism. If the only requisite for holiness is to know that one is a sinner, would this not mean that virtue is a temptation to self-complacency and sin the most secure and evangelical of all states?

So by a singular paradox the same men who undermine the foundation of Christian holiness by destroying all courageous effort, at the same time blame Christians for not being saints. A choice must be made. In this there is no question of morality. " Because, " as Péguy said, " morality was invented by malingerers and Christian life by Jesus Christ. " This is a question of Christian life and of holiness. Now it is through the day by day effort to be faithful to prayer, to work, to purity, it is through one's awkward efforts, it is through the willed acceptance of what is crippling, it is through the irony of worldliness, it is through the bad example of Christians that holiness is acquired.

Maritain says : " The world demands saints. " This is true. The world does not reproach Christians because they are Christian but because they are not sufficiently Christian. There can be no doubt that the very men who ridicule Christians, deep down within themselves, envy them their faith. Today the world is looking for Christians shining with the glory of the risen Christ, in whom the Holy Spirit is perfecting His wonderful works and whose holiness is a proof of divine grace's sovereign power.

* * *

In saying this are we not considering the problem merely on the personal plane? Surely what the world wants most today is help in solving its problems. Is this the moment to be concerned about its holiness when so many temporal tasks clamor for attention? Is it really true that the world asks us to be saints? Is it not asking instead that we give it bread, that we struggle against injustice, that we work for peace? When we talk about holiness are we not in danger of neglecting the service of our brothers?

This objection must be faced frankly. The charge is a serious one. We must remember that we are speaking of the holiness of laymen, not of the holiness of monks. We are considering men whose lives are spent performing temporal duties. We are considering the fact that the demands

15

of professional life, political life and social life never cease. We know that the Church insistently summons us to these tasks. And this, more urgently than ever before, because Christians are needed in the shaping of the world.

Does the Church contradict itself? Here again we face a serious problem. Practically speaking, the difficulty comes from the fact that it is hard to reconcile the exigencies of personal sanctification and the exigencies of temporal tasks. It is also difficult because some men today set these two domains in opposition one with the other. On one side they show us the domain of faith in which are to be found eternal things. On the other side they point to the domain of events, where no law prevails but that of the meaning of present history which is conditioned by men's skill. The logical conclusion is that there is a basic dualism in our lives.

Against such a concept we must protest. The vocation to holiness is in no way opposed to the vocation to temporal tasks. First of all there is no danger that holiness will turn us away from temporal tasks. There is no danger of any exclusive concentration on the divine because God could never lead us away from the service of our brothers. Quite the contrary, it is near God that the Christian finds strength to perform with faith and courage the tasks that are his. It is in prayer that we discover the selflessness of love. It is in prayer that one of the most daring and the most effective men of our time, Giorgio La Pira, draws his courage and his enthusiasm.

There is one thing that no one can ever make me believe. It is that Christians have failed to fulfill their obligations to society because they are too much concerned about God. The truth is that they have failed in their social obligations because they have not been concerned about God. The temporal well-being of the world has nothing to fear from the conversion of Christians. Christians do not have to be converted to the world. That form of conversion takes care of itself. What must be done is to convert Christians to God. Then they will in truth devote themselves to their brothers. Becoming a saint is not dangerous. Or rather, there is a danger, but the danger affects us and no one else; a saint must practice greater charity.

This should be expressed even more emphatically. Holiness not only does not prevent the layman from performing his temporal tasks, it exacts heroic obedience to God's will which becomes the dynamic of his temporal action, because the goal of action in time is to establish justice and peace among men. Now to be a Christian is to do this, to act because this is God's will and God's will is absolute in its exactions. It is precisely this articulation of temporal action with the divine law that many Christians now no longer see. It is only when a Christian understands temporal activity in this light that it becomes for him a duty binding in conscience, no matter what the cost. Holiness in this sense for a layman would mean the fulfillment, in family and society, of God's will at the price of any sacrifice. Perhaps this will be the way in which Christians will be able to do something for the world.

Finally, I want to affirm that these human tasks, performed in obedience to God, will also be for the layman the path that leads him to God. Here, again, we must deny, this time on the interior plane, that any opposition exists between the temporal and the spiritual. Some Christians think that temporal action is necessarily profane. Therefore to be a layman means that a man gives up the idea of being a saint, that he resigns himself to mediocrity. True it is, that there is an unacceptable dualism as long as the idea persists that the providential tasks that God gives us hinder the sanctification of our souls. As a matter of fact it is these temporal tasks that become the means of our holiness. This they are indeed when we carry them out as we would the divine will, performing them obediently and lovingly, accepting all the mortification they bring with them.

* * *

We have reached the point where we may formulate our conclusion in these words: holiness is the only problem. The immediate drama is the presence in the world of so many baptized men and women, so many Christians who are not faithful to their vocation to holiness. The drama is the drama of mediocrity. A Church which is a Church of saints would change the world. First of all, and this is its primary task, it would convert the world, just as a few apostles converted the ancient world, just as the great saints have done, a Paul, a Francis Xavier, a Vincent Ferrer. But such a Church would also affect the world's temporal destiny through the generosity it would arouse, through the light it would radiate. The task that is ours is to create a human order worthy of love, in whose heart men can realize a vocation that is divine. This is the task which the world looks to Christians to perform. They will perform it only if, first of all, according to their own vocation, according to their own profession, they strive humbly, but faithfully to become saints.

Love
of God

2

Love of neighbor is one of Christ's chief commandments : " By this shall all men know that you are my disciples, if you have love one for another. " This mark ought to distinguish the Christian community. That it does not, constitutes the gravest of scandals. How will unbelievers recognize the face of Christ in a community where charity has grown cold? About this Péguy was correct. If great numbers of men have turned away from the Church in the last two centuries, it is not because Christian dogmas have been broken down by newly invented pseudo-arguments, but it is " because what remains today of the Christian world is so lacking in charity. " For this reason two of the most precious signs of the present vitality of Catholicism are the quickening spirit of charity and the renewal of communal life. But as sometimes happens, certain groups, stressing this aspect of Christianity (as they have every right to do), have tried to concentrate on it too exclusively. As a result the total concept is distorted. Do not misunderstand me. This could never be the result of any excess in the practice of charity! [1] " The only measure of love is to love without measure. " Here we refer to an idea of charity that many men hold today. When they allege that charity is the only precept, we must guard against the danger of allowing charity to seem self-sufficient. The next step would be an easy one, and it would be to confuse Gospel charity with every form of neighborly love. To do this is to reduce the Gospel to a message of human brotherhood. Wherever men discovered this fraternal spirit they labeled it Christianity. Some men were pleased to exalt the Gospel character of certain political or ideological communities by way of contrast with the so-called formalism of the Church.

I need not point out that there is often much that is unjust in such accusations. Nor are we about to absolve the Christian world from its serious failures against charity. Nevertheless we must admit the continuing presence of much hidden charity in the Church, in religious orders, in charitable organizations, even in everyday life. But this is not our objective. What we intend to do is to uncover the error that consists in seeing the charity of Christ wherever there is a human community spirit, even when God is far from the community. Now if charity is the test of an authentic love of God, as Saint Augustine has proved in his masterful way, love of neighbor in no way

[1] Unless otherwise specified, in this whole chapter the word charity means only charity towards one's neighbor.

24

constitutes a dispensation from this love of God. Nor could it ever replace this love. Nevertheless we often find that this substitution is made and to do so is to make charity a word without a meaning because a love for men which does not flow from a love for God, in no sense deserves to be called charity.

* * *

Christianity is a totality whose different parts are delicately balanced. This is true in the order of dogma. Heresy always consists in stressing one point and neglecting the rest. This is also true in the practical order. It may happen that love of God is exalted at the expense of love of neighbor. We know how specious and how pharisaical may be the pretexts by which truth is defended against charity. We also know that we may mistake an effort to satisfy subtle forms of selfishness for an effort to attain to union with God. Love of God is not free from illusions. But this loss of equilibrium can work in the opposite direction. Today this is the greater and surely the more frequent danger. Therefore, it is of this danger that we speak.

In this case, to disturb the balance is to establish a false perspective. Then Christianity's center of interest will be found in the human collectivity, and man's relations with God will be pushed in the background. Certainly this in no way means that we deny the second aspect. But this does not lessen the danger of deforming the Christian message. The first commandment is always to love God. The first conversion is man's recognition that he is not of himself and that all that he is, he has received from Another. It is this acknowledgement that constitutes the primordial religious act in which man freely ratifies his condition as creature. It is this act that touches the most intimate part of his being, reaching the passion of the possession of one's self and of being sufficient unto one's self which constitutes the very essence of sin — and it is the fundamental act of dispossession that opens man to the life of love.

The conversion of man to God is the Church's first mission. The first inspiration of this missionary spirit will always be found in the effort to have God's name hallowed, His kingdom come, His will done. For this reason the apostolate supposes adoration, love of neighbor, love of God. For this reason in seeking to extend God's reign over the hearts of men, the Church is assuring at the same time their true happiness. Saint Irenaeus understood this when he wrote : " Man's life is the vision of God. " What is established outside of God is a world of death, according to the teaching of Saint Paul. For man to open himself to God is to live; it is to restore him to his true being.

Now it is just this fundamental theocentricity of Christianity which some Christians today seem to have lost. Certain phases of this deviation may be traced. It is rooted in a false interpretation of the work of Christ. The Incarnation ceases to be the descent of the Word of God to fallen human nature in order to restore it to its divine orientation; today, on the contrary, for some the term denotes a shift of accent from God to man. The Incarnation is seen as the engagement in human reality through which man realizes his plenitude. We will see the abuses this word occasions when it is used by some non-Christian authors. A communist like Garaudy can write in *Antée* that " it was the day that he became a party member that he understood the Christian mystery of the Incarnation. " Merleau-Ponty says that " the Christianity of the Incarnation " has transferred to man the attributes that " the Christianity of transcendence " had ascribed to God. Jung sees in the redemption " the reparation of a divine injustice to the human being. "

Thus the Incarnation is said to be God's recognition of man's greatness. " If God came in the flesh He did so in order to share in every human joy. There is no human being who can claim to be human as long as he limits in any way his will to total happiness. " [1] As a result, Christians are reproached because they do not open themselves to human values. They are urged to be converted to the world and to love this earth. They are allowed only as much of Christianity as can bring them human enrichment. We know to what disasters an attitude like this can lead. When the situation changes, when God's will requires sacrifice, when it is a question of giving up a certain human happiness or of obeying the dictates of the Church, there will be conflict. This is inevitable.

To shift the emphasis in this way has important consequences in the practical order. First

[1] Jean MASSIN, *Le festin chez Lévi*, p. 26.

of all, any " theocentric " appraisal of Christianity will be brutally devaluated. If the first way of looking at Christianity is to see it in terms of man's union with man, then the soul's personal relation with God, as it is expressed in a life of prayer, will be stripped of all meaning. God will be sought " in others. " Every manifestation of religious life will be made in common. This is not to underestimate the great value of the renewal of community life which characterizes our time and which has renewed Christian life in many ways. But if this aspect becomes exclusive, it impoverishes. If the Church is the place where the greatest communion of souls is made possible, it must also at the same time be the place of great solitudes. Père Clérissac used to say that the Church is both Desert and City. A Christian world that had lost the meaning of the contemplative life would be mutilated and cut in half. Without personal prayer there can be no Christian life.

Not only is the importance of personal prayer misunderstood, at times it is even regarded with suspicion. Interior life is seen as a kind of evasion, a form of isolation, a waste of energy. We are willing to admit, as we have said, that the interior life is difficult and that in it illusions are possible. To be more precise, there are forms of interior life which are simply man's effort to find himself by creating inner silence. These efforts can be good. They may also be a form of self-seeking and bespeak a subtle egoism. But there is nothing like this in Christian prayer. There is no danger that it will ever isolate us from others. It is a turning in upon self so that we find God in His dwelling place within the soul. Contact like this with God will have no other result than to give us a better love for others.

I speak advisedly when I say : a better love. Because the danger that we are describing here is not only to stress love of neighbor at the expense of the love of God, it is also by way of result to falsify the Christian meaning of love of neighbor. In the measure that love of neighbor flows from the love of God, it enables us to see others as God sees them. Each man seems to us to be a certain idea of God, a certain imitation of His beauty, a certain masterpiece on which He is at work. Charity then becomes a cooperation with God the worker. It is a working with Him to raise up the city of the Sons of God. Christian charity embraces the whole man, but precisely because it embraces him totally, it sees him in what gives him his fullness, in his eternal vocation.

Cut off from the love of God, charity will drop to a merely human level of solidarity. Admittedly there is solidarity like this outside Christianity. History is full of examples of men devoted to other men on the human level. We, too, are surrounded with examples. In Christianity itself, this temporal charity plays an essential role, both on the level of the individual as well as on the level of society. Christ's charity is all-inclusive. But precisely because it is all-inclusive, it cannot stop short when it finds bodily misery; because beyond this there is another kind of misery, one that is far worse and that is spiritual misery. Only Christ went to the lowest depths of all misery, because He alone descended into the realm of Death in order to destroy the power of death. What a loss, then, it is for Christians to reduce their message to terms of temporal freedom which must always be limited!

Furthermore, only with difficulty does human solidarity escape certain restrictions. It tends to concentrate exclusively on a privileged group to the exclusion of all others. It tends to become devotion to the workers' world or to national freedom. Where God is not the only absolute, it is very difficult for men not to take as absolutes the human causes to which they devote themselves. Devotedness there will then be, but it will be devotedness to idols. Nazism inspired fanatical devotedness. The most abandoned of causes have had heroes. Some people are inclined to see charity present wherever man's devotedness reaches the point of sacrifice. This is to forget, as Clement of Alexandria long ago observed, that what gives value to a sacrifice is not the renouncement that it evokes, but the quality of the love by which it is inspired.

Perhaps it is because some Christians today fail to recognize this, that it is possible for them to accept so lightly the idea of the victory of communism. In fact, if we stay on the level of a concept of charity that seeks only man's temporal liberation, such an attitude is understandable; even though the least that can be said is that it is a debatable point whether or not communism is a liberation even on the temporal plane. But if to love men means first of all to wish them the highest good, which is God, can a Christian responsible for souls, balance, even for an instant, the few temporal advantages which communism might possibly represent, against the immense spiritual loss which would follow? That such a question can be raised proves to what a point the true idea of charity, cut off from its divine roots, has been perverted.

* * *

So far we have stated the danger of a false concept of charity which deflects Christianity from its basic orientation towards God and at the same time perverts the very order of human relationships. To state this danger is not enough; we must also explain it. Such a reversal of perspectives does not come about without reason. Now these causes seem to be certain changes in the modern conscience which are both the expression of valid sociological findings and the conclusions of false ideologies — and their pressure makes itself felt in the very heart of Christianity : a conscious awareness of the social nature of human existence, a desire for an effective revolution of economic changes, man's discovery of the power science gives him : these are so many power-ideas which tend to shift the axis of theological charity.

A little while ago we said that one of the ways in which charity is falsely defined today is to say that it is merely man's awareness of his union with man. Such a statement could only be formulated because it expresses the fundamental experience of our time. It is linked with obvious

31

sociological factors and especially with increasing interdependence of men with men in the field of economic relations. This economic fact has created a new type of humanism which may be called social humanism, and whose chief affirmation is that the human value of the individual depends on the state of society in which man finds himself. It follows, therefore, that " man is man only in community with other men. " The Marxist interpretation of this statement is unilateral and materialistic : this community with others is that which is expressed in economic relations and so it is in the realization of these true economic ties that the human essence is realized.

No matter what may be the pattern of these distortions, it remains true that this awareness is the expression on the human level of a basic fact of our times, namely the crisis of economic individualism as it is found in liberal capitalism. This crisis was not only economic, it is also moral. Economic individualism engendered moral individualism. The bourgeois world was a world of isolation. This isolation became intolerable. This is why the discovery of an economic community in which man is united with man seemed to many men to be the deliverance for which they were waiting. To this worker's world, where social humanism is best expressed, it brought the message as it were of a new birth, because it made possible man's union with man in a world weary of individualistic humanism.

It is a blessed and established fact that this reawakening of the sense of community in the contemporary world has helped Christians to rediscover certain poorly understood aspects of their faith. The renewal of the theology of the Mystical Body, the liturgical movement and Catholic Action are some of its manifestations. But it also made possible the danger of interpreting these Christian realities as functions of modern conceptions of the human community and of confusing conversion to Christianity with awareness of human solidarity. Christianity is a life of charity : it is also acceptance of Christian dogmas and reception of the sacraments. It is a serious matter that some men could reach the conclusion that they could reject these elements, yet preserve what is essential in Christianity. [1]

It is not out of place here to describe the ways that such men have twisted the dogma of the Mystical Body. They have understood it to be the Christian expression of the experience of human solidarity. From Saint Paul they have taken the idea of the interdependence of the members, but in doing this, their perspective was faulty. Pius XII recalled in the Encyclical *Mystici Corporis*, that what is primary in the Pauline doctrine of the Mystical Body is the relation of the members to the Head. Only insofar as the members are united to Christ are they united to each other. Christ is the bond of their unity. He is also the measure. They are brought back to the relation of man with God which constitutes Christian charity. It is precisely this element that has not

[1] Cf. Louis BOUYER, " Où en est la Théologie du Corps Mystique, " *Rev. Sciences Religieuses*, 1948, p. 326.

been understood. It is man's relation with Christ which gives Christian charity a depth and dimension that is divine.

There are practical consequences to this truth. One of the reasons why, in some places today, there are few vocations to the priesthood, is that many fear " to up-root themselves, " " to cut themselves off from men. " It is true that a priest is a man apart. It is also true that in this sense Christ does separate, and that He comes carrying a sword. But if He breaks the bonds of the corporal community, bonds of work, of place, of race, it is to lead us to a deeper union situated on the level of the communion of saints, on the level of a community that is spiritual. This can result in a certain loss of human fellowship. But the new bonds which will be created are of a greatness that is altogether different. Membership in an ecclesiastical community and in a worker's community are not in the same category and are not to be compared.

A further essential aspect of Gospel charity also contributes to the confusion. Charity is essentially efficacious. " Let us not love in word, neither with the tongue, but in deed and in truth, " said Saint John. Love for God is creative. It expresses itself in effective service that is costly and real. It means to edify, that is to build the city of souls.

Charity to be effective today must express itself in human terms. It must take part in revolutionary action against a world in which economic institutions and political injustices condemn a large part of mankind to a life of misery. The first cause of this state of things is the faulty division of wealth which Popes have often condemned. Against this social injustice men have risen from every class. But it must be acknowledged that most of these men belong to a non-Christian world and that Christians too often have supported and now support a set-up which benefits them, without troubling themselves to examine whether these conditions are a violation of justice and consequently whether they are contrary to God's law.

This explains the shock caused in certain consciences by the discovery of this contradiction. From Ozanam to Albert de Mun, from Mounier to the young people active in Catholic Action today, this attitude has been the mark of the best in contemporary Christianity. Besides it is nothing more than the expression of the most formal will of the Church. What must weigh heavily upon us is that this attitude, in the last analysis, has had no influence on many who officially claim to be Catholics. The Christian layman's duty of " temporal engagement, " that is, of effective contact with the world in which he lives, is an essential part of his Christian vocation. It is in the name of his Christianity that he is bound to bring about in society the reign of an order which respects the law of God, which permits the development of human persons, which establishes just relations in economic life.

Here, again, the anxiety for what is temporally efficacious has brought about a displacement in the order of charity which falsifies its basic meaning. In this displacement it is possible to distinguish different degrees. Often the economic liberation of the temporal city is stressed almost exclusively and the primary character of the spiritual liberation of the heavenly city is underestimated. The spiritual means by which the heavenly city is to be built will be valued less, as the efficacy of the temporal efforts are the more obvious. Men will build a Christian civilization and they will make this their final end instead of establishing God's kingdom which is rooted in the Church. To work done in the field of labor or politics they will assign a higher value than the work of the missionary apostolate.

Of even greater moment is the fact that this building up of a temporal society will disguise a mystic meaning. No longer will it be merely a matter of working concretely to suppress certain injustices or certain miseries. Men will adopt the myth of the coming of an earthly paradise where liberated mankind will live in prosperity and peace. Revolutionary activity will assume the nature of an absolute. The working class will appear invested in a messianic role, as if it were capable of regenerating human society. Marxism will shine with a mystic radiance in Christian minds that it never enjoyed in the minds of the founders of scientific socialism. This false mysticism incompatible with man's present condition which is always limited and with the ambiguity necessarily inherent in institutions of a world in which sin exists is one of the most regrettable deviations of certain thinkers.

Temporal charity considered from a more practical point of view will take priority over spiritual charity, not because of their relative values, but because of an urgent need. To preach the Gospel in a world of perverted economics will be deemed futile — besides being old-fashioned. First destroy what is bad. Then Christianity can be erected on new foundations. Moreover since communism seems to be the only power able to crush capitalism and may well be the blueprint of the society of tomorrow, Christians will be told that it is their duty to collaborate with communists. Once the victory is won, time enough then to establish the rights of a religious man.

We must examine one last way in which, it seems to us, contemporary social humanism has falsified the true concept of charity. This brings us back to what seems to be the essential point: the danger of failing to see the primacy of the love for God over the love for the neighbor. In fact it is a characteristic of humanism today for man to pretend to a certain self-sufficiency. This is found in the atheistic existentialism of a Sartre in an individualistic form. In Marxism it appears in the power of human society to establish itself apart from God, in man's unaided power to achieve his own liberation. Religion is seen to be an estrangement which, by not placing in God the center of gravity, empties man of his very substance.

It is clear that Christians cannot state the problem so radically. They will not deny that God exists. But they will distinguish the sphere of religion in which man depends on God from the temporal domain where man is autonomous and self-sufficient. They will justify the presence in the world of the spiritual man but they will not allow his intervention in the temporal domain. They would declare that it would be an abuse of power were the Church to intervene here. This charge strikes at the root of the Christian position. If it is obvious that what is purely technical in economic and social life springs from science alone, it is also true that God's domain is universal and God's law binds societies as well as individuals. Those who hold the theory which we are criticizing, have not sufficiently observed that in freeing revolutionaries from God's law, they have also freed conservatives, and that they who hold this theory not only forfeit the right to criticize those others from the Christian point of view, but that they themselves meet half way the motives which inspired them.

Not only will the autonomy of temporal action in relation to a transcendent reference be reaffirmed but a warning will be given against the danger of estrangement that this reference might represent, in leading to " a lack of respect for human things. " How unexpected is this necessity in which a man, especially a layman, finds that he must defend himself from estrangement from God. Precisely a reference to God is the only reference which could never constitute an estrangement but which, on the contrary, alone gives meaning to human realities if their essence is to be created. How can it be said, in the field of practical experience, that the fact all things are directed to God ever turned men from their human tasks, if these human tasks were truly their God-given vocation?

* * *

We can conclude. There is a growing tendency among some of our contemporaries to find the essence of Christianity in man's relation with man. They reason that wherever this human communion exists, there is Christianity. Love of neighbor may sometimes unknowingly be love of God. It may also remain on a purely human plane, far from any love of God. It may even be in conscious opposition to God. Perhaps modern man's last temptation is a desire to show that without God it is possible to do good. Antichrist will be, in Claudel's profound insight, " he in whom mankind reunited and consolidated can say to the Word : We have no more need of Thee. " [1]

To say this is not to set limits to the basic affirmation that charity to the neighbor is the sign by which Christ wishes His disciples to be recognized. To refuse to allow neighborly love to be reduced to a sentiment of human community, is to exalt it, not to lessen it. It is to refuse to limit it to the natural plane in order to give it a dimension that is divine. Love is the life of the triune God. In Christ this love communicates itself

[1] The exact opposite of Claudel's position is taken by his old disciple, M. Jean MASSIN : " In the measure that the Christian sees that a growing number of unbelievers show a more active charity than he for mankind's daily needs, does he multiply calls upon transcendence to convince himself that the purely human benevolence of the Good Shepherd is diabolic "; *Le festin chez Lévi*, p. 212.

so that it can take possession of men and lift them to the life of God. It is this relation with God which alone gives charity its dimension. To want to confine, diminish or hide the divine origin and goal of all true charity is to destroy what gives it its fullness. This is why we have thought it necessary to recall that love of the neighbor is the second commandment. Love of God is the first. Without the first, there can be no second.

Obedience

3

The increased importance of laymen is one of the striking facts of the last thirty years in the life of the Church. This has created new problems. The layman's position is not always a comfortable one. He finds himself at a point where two worlds meet. Baptism makes him a member of a Church in which he plays an active role and where his actions are essentially religious. At the same time his professional, political and economic activities involve him in a temporal society. In this society is he to be concerned only about his fellow men? Is his attitude to be that of a Christian? In a certain sense the Church asks of him initiative and efficiency. But this does not mean that he is perfectly free. As a result there are men who find this position disturbing.

In our eyes this is one of the day's great problems. How hard it is to reconcile the demands of life in labor or industry with the demands of religion. Is there no answer? We would like to suggest what is at least an outline of an anwer, and to show the exact point where man's temporal commitments impinge upon his spiritual life.

We can begin with a temptation confronting some Christians today. I shall describe it as a kind of hopelessness about the ability of Christianity to do anything about the temporal order. To give us divine life through the Sacraments, to nourish our faith with sermons — this is expected of the Church — but nothing along the lines of improving the earthly city. Such are the thoughts of many young Christians who, at first, concentrated almost too exclusively on the social aspect of Christianity. They have been disappointed. In their reaction they have gone to the opposite extreme.

Of course, we cannot deny that it is well to stress the fact that it is the role of the Church to lead us to the City that is to come, that Christianity is meant to introduce us to a world quite different from that of the temporal city — but, although we cannot deny this, we think that on this point there is something more to be said. As a matter of fact, in a certain sense it is dangerous to say that Christianity's chief purpose was the improvement of the earthly city. To say this is to reduce Christianity to a temporal messianism and at the same time to take away its essential message. The Church has reminded us (at the time of the *Sillon*) that the Gospel cannot be identified with any kind of political society whatsoever.

Here we are considering something quite different. If men insist that there be a sharp cleavage between the earthly city and the city that is above, they do so, less through fear that the supernatural end of Christianity shall become a merely temporal ideal, than through fear that man's purely human tasks will suffer through contact with what is transcendent. Here we must be very exact in expressing what we mean.

We do not deny that there is a danger of misunderstanding the proper order of human tasks. Appeal to the supernatural may be an invalid dispensation from human effort. Péguy found masterful formulas to express this : " He who makes use of prayer and Sacrament to dispense himself from work and action (this is the equivalent of not fighting during a war), breaks the order established by God Himself, and he breaks the oldest of all commandments. " [1]

It is also correct to say that the development of civilization has enabled man to enter and control sphere after sphere which, through their very inaccessibility, were once believed to be supernatural. Christians have not been alone in doing this. In a general way men of ancient times sought supernatural help in the case of illnesses which were beyond their power to cure, and for which today appeal would first be made to medical science. To quote a recent author : " Man has the right and even the duty, in purely human matters, to trust himself. " [2]

[1] L'Argent, suite; Œuvres complètes, XIV, 241.
[2] R. A. GAUTHIER, La Magnanimité, p. 493.

In the political order this is equally true. To ensure the stability of the temporal city, the ancient world conferred a sacred character upon political institutions. This is the sacral type of society which Maritain has so well defined. Such was the Roman empire. Such is Islam today. Such were the medieval states. In the last example, as Father Victor White has clearly seen : " Christianity was used as the religion of a sacral society. " [1]

This kind of society had serious disadvantages. " It was, " as Father White remarks, " from the sacral intolerance of the Roman Empire that Christianity suffered, and from it alone. " There is in fact a danger of giving an absolute value to political technics, and of confusing what is right for the state with what is orthodox in religion.

Therefore it is entirely correct to state that a more technical way of considering political and social institutions, one that stresses the autonomy of the temporal city in its own order, not only is not contrary to right order but is really a proof of progress. The Church found it necessary to exercise political power at a time when the state alone was unable to maintain order in the city. But such a situation was not meant to last. A more adult society quite naturally tries to provide its own organization. In this there is a correct distinction of order that can but be mutually advantageous to Church and state.

But to restore human technics to domains where they rightly belong is altogether

[1] Dogme et tolérance, *Evidence*, November 1953, p. 4.

different from claiming an autonomy for forms of human activity, which would withdraw this activity from its basic orientation to God. What is restored to man on the sacral plane is not taken away from God. Temporal action, rightly exercised in domains which correspond to the reality of things, may be withdrawn from the Church's direct jurisdiction but this action does not thereby become autonomous, nor does it cease to be fundamentally directed to God, either in the line of subject (man's reason for acting is always obedience to God), or in the line of objects (for in the last analysis objects are always means in relation to man's unique and final end).

It seems to me that Father Gauthier does not recognize this, when, after remarking quite accurately that " progress is the distinguishing mark between the ecclesiastical sphere and the temporal sphere, " he continues : " The Fathers concentrated all their attention on God and they elaborated a spirituality of immediate adhesion to God . . . The drama of the modern world began in the sixteenth and seventeenth centuries when by an inexorable process, autonomy was restored to secular institutions but at the same time, Christian spirituality was returning to an outdated Augustinianism. " [1]

To say this is to confuse the legitimately independent action of temporal institutions in their contacts with ecclesiastical society, and man's illegitimately independent action in relation to his supernatural end.

[1] *La Magnanimité*, p. 497.

It is this last position that is dangerous today. A distinction is rightly made between the transcendent and the temporal, but it is not recognized that this distinction becomes dangerous as soon as the hierarchy of the transcendent and the temporal is no longer respected. There are certain extremists who have reached this conclusion. " In modern society faith in God has ceased to be the motive of man's efforts to attain his own destiny. What then can he do? In his ardent desire to better the world in which he finds himself he can become the link with another world where, through grace, he is equally at home. "[1] It is true that man belongs to two worlds : the world of God and the world of man. But as a matter of fact, once these two worlds are separated, man's only concern is for this present world.

This attitude is basically unsound. The idea that a reference to God can endanger human values and that they should be considered as they are in themselves, seems to claim that religion is a grave danger today.

While in past centuries the right of the Church to intervene in temporal matters was often challenged, now it is man's dependence on God Himself that is questioned. On the contrary, the meaning of human realities can come only from their relation to God, if it is of their essence to be created, and if everything on earth is but a means to enable man to achieve his only end which is to glorify God.

[1] " Dieu, pourquoi faire? " *Jeunesse de l'Eglise*, XI, p. 131.

This also seems to us to be a serious error in the practical order. To consider man's temporal activities apart from their reference to God is to remove the chief dynamic from his action because the obligation to act becomes imperative only insofar as it touches the domain of conscience, that is to say when it is a question of good and evil. Now the law of good and evil is God's will. Far from being able to suppose that the Christian will become more efficient in the temporal order when he no longer refers to God, it must be admitted that Christianity would have had greater influence on social institutions if we had always had the courage to show that obedience to God, as an absolute duty, affects man's whole temporal, political, professional and family life. If Christians have not been more revolutionary, it is not because they lacked freedom but because they have not been sufficiently obedient.

This does not mean that we must mix the ecclesiastical and the temporal order, but it does mean that we must affirm that even on the temporal plane, man's activity depends on God and has as its highest norm the glory of God. Father de Montcheuil has well remarked :

> There is a whole temporal order that is not the eternal order. This order does not concern the Church, who is not charged with advancing its construction. Does it follow that the Church has nothing to say about it? To answer affirmatively is to answer too hastily. The Church rules the Christian directly. But the Christian remains a man. It is the same being who leads both a natural and a supernatural

49

life, using, so to speak, the same instruments. It is with the same will that he loves God and confronts human objectives. It is impossible to lead two totally separate lives : a Christian life and a human life.

Political or social engagement is, for the Christian, an answer to a divine call. Jacques Maritain described in his masterful way these saints of the temporal order, " freed from all but Jesus, " facing the difficult situation of the modern world and drawing from prayer the strength and light to perform their difficult tasks. Only men freed from all bonds can give an integral answer to the demands of the Gospel and refuse all entanglements. It is in these demands that the Christian will find the leaven that can transform society. Only to the extent that Christian laymen are united to God will they be faithful. For it is from this union with God that the layman as well as the religious will draw, each according to his vocation, a love of the divine will that can make them capable of an obedience that may go so far as heroism.

Obedience to God is therefore to be found at the beginning of the Christian's temporal obligations. It is also at the end. The temporal city is not a final end, it is directed to the supernatural city. In the light of this last end the Christian considers improvements of the temporal city. In this perspective he seeks to establish an order where men can realize their divine vocation as fully as possible. The material conditions of men's lives must be such that they can lead a spiritual life. This is another instance where we can see how far fidelity can lead. This also supposes an order in which the Church is free to realize the mission given to it by God for all men and for which it is answerable to God.

Nor is this all. The temporal city would not be so cut off from the spiritual community that it would fail to be penetrated with its spirit. Although the Gospel provides no formula for the international allocation of gasoline and suggests no salary scale, nevertheless the effective organization of the temporal city ought even here below faintly to foreshadow the kingdom of God. Ricœur has clearly shown how eschatology gives a prophetic note to the Christian's temporal action.

> The bond that unites faith with politics is a bond of inspiration or intention. Faith gives a total perspective for profane thoughts or acts. On the plane of institutions, of kinds of work, of property, I must show that love of God and love of neighbor are one. In my search for economic and social justice I find a symbol of my longing for the coming of the kingdom of God.... Christians must first seek to maintain the tension of a faltering history and to renew its revolutionary perspective by their own prophetic vehemence. [1]

Here we see how artificial is the opposition often made today between a social Christianity and an eschatological Christianity. This opposition is to be found only where Christianity is failing. But all Christianity is primarily and necessarily eschatological in the measure that this eschatological perspective also means the ordination

---

[1] *Les Chrétiens et la Politique*, p. 87.

of temporal society and the Christian's temporal engagements to this end. Here again we see how the separation of the two domains deprives the temporal action of the Christian of its essential motive and its measure. Without eschatological expectations, social Christianity ceases to be effective.

It is now clear that obedience to God in any action affecting temporal institutions will express itself in an effort to further the reign of charity. This is the object of Christ's explicit command : " My commandment is that you love one another. " Repeatedly the Church reminds us of obedience to this command.

> How will the Church intervene in the temporal order? The Church will necessarily remind us of the law of charity which must everywhere prevail. Usually this reminder will not contain definite applications to be made to institutions at a given moment. That effort is left to our initiative. . . . Nevertheless all man's temporal activity must be affected by Christ. With his whole mind and with all his strength, the Christian must discover and use the means that will bring about, on the temporal plane, the ideal of charity and of communion which the Church has taught him. [1]

So it is that an all-loving obedience to the divine will is, in our eyes, the dynamic which is essential to the Christian's temporal activity. This is what Marx would call faith in man. [2] This obedience is found at the origin of

[1] MONTCHEUIL, *L'Église et le monde moderne*, p. 131.
[2] *Chronique Sociale*, 1938, pp. 280-281.

all human acts, and gives them their moral character, that is it considers them in relation to God. This obedience is found at their goal, which is the effective ordering of all things to man's last end and is the binding nature of the commandment of charity. This commandment is found in the divine will and is its expression. Here the human community is not the determining principle but the fact that this community is willed by God and that this will is an absolute.

Is all this not rather general? Does it not leave the Christian with almost no guidance when he must make definite decisions? This brings us to our last and important problem. It is remarkable that on this point the Church is sometimes blamed because it interferes in areas where it has no jurisdiction, sometimes because it does not take sides in conflicts between man and man, thus giving an impression of indifference. First, a distinction must be made. Although the Church quite rightfully recognizes the legitimacy of many political or economic institutions, nevertheless it may only intervene in this domain insofar as the final end makes such intervention desirable. While there is nothing properly dogmatic about interventions of this kind, they are an expression of the Church's mission to direct the temporal activity of Christians to the goal that we have tried to describe.

It is clear even in this extreme case that the Church is not to make the individual's responsibility its own. There is and there ought to be a wide undefined area where legitimate differences can find expression, where initiative has free play because the Church protects the Christian's rightful liberty in the temporal domain. The Church does not leave him entirely alone because it indicates the broad outlines of his work. But it does ask him to devise the technical solutions which will transform theory into fact. If it is dangerous to challenge the right of the Church to any form of intervention in this domain, it is equally dangerous to wait idly until the Church has acted, and meanwhile to dispense ourselves from any initiative.

This is the situation of the Christian layman. It is impossible to consider his temporal engagement apart from his obedience to God. It is impossible to consider that his obedience to God dispenses him from any effort. Will it be said that this is asking too much and too little? Too much, if this implies that the Christian is to judge every temporal engagement in the light of God's law and the teaching of the Church. Too little, if the Church does not provide him with a ready-made solution for this or that special problem. It is precisely this dilemma, this difficult situation that men seek to avoid either by emancipation or passivity but which, on the contrary, forces the Christian to act as a creature, that is to be at once obedient and free, faithful and creative.

Thus we come to the final question. It is this : In spite of all we say, if we stress obedience, do we not favor conservative and reactionary tendencies? Do we not preach a gospel of resignation which may serve as a screen behind which established powers can continue their oppression? Has not the law of work often been invoked in the past to force laboring masses to accept their servitude so that they may enrich an aristocracy of idlers, happy that the work of others makes possible their own dispensation? Has not the divine character of the hierarchy of society and authority been made a rampart in order to defend against revolutionary assaults powers which were in fact unjust?

True, obedience today seems to be a lost virtue. Since the eighteenth century, believers in progress preach a doctrine of emancipation. Liberty is the watchword of all who claim to be working for the coming of a better society. I will not insist on the easily verified paradox that has led liberty's defenders to establish the most totalitarian states that the world has ever seen. Obedience unrecognized, turns up where least expected. But I will observe that obedience is held in low repute even by Catholics. Christianity's message of liberation alone is well received. No longer fashionable is the old saying: To serve God is to reign. Men even deny that obedience is a gospel virtue, preferring to see in it only a requirement for the common good.

Here I need not establish the gospel foundations of Christian obedience; [1] I shall consider merely the reproach leveled against obedience that it fosters passivity. Now what I deny is that obedience is devoted to the service of tradition rather than to revolution, to the establishment of order rather than to the order to be established. It was in the name of obedience that Old Testament

---

[1] H. HOLSTEIN, " Le mystère de l'obéissance, " *Etudes*, September 1953, pp. 7 ff.

prophets rose up against the injustice of their times. It is enough to recall the well known and timely passage from Isaias : " Woe to you that join house to house and lay field to field, even to the end of the place : shall you alone dwell in the midst of the earth? " (5 : 8). The whole book of *Amos* is a protest against social and international injustice : deportation (1 : 6), the selling into slavery of insolvent debtors (2 : 6), the increase of the wealth of some and the consequent impoverishment of others (5 : 11).

Perhaps we shall be told that these are merely examples of the sociological reality of the class struggle, and that similar phenomena are to be observed in Greece and Rome.

Speaking of Amos, A. Neher wrote : " This scene may take its place in history as an episode of the pitiless struggle in which, through the centuries, the poor have risen against the rich, revolution against tyranny, the demagogue against power. Amos becomes the politician. " [1] And he quotes Renan : " The prophet of the eighth century is an out-of-door journalist, declaiming his article. His first concern is to impress the people. To succeed, the prophet does not fail to resort to all the tricks modern publicists think they have invented. " [2]

Certainly Amos is very much of a revolutionary. No man has ever spoken more vehemently against established discorder, against injustice, against the belittlement of man. But his

[1] *Amos, Contribution à l'histoire du prophétisme*, 1950, p. 156.
[2] *Histoire du peuple d'Israël*, II, 422.

revolution is not made in the name of any human ideal, whatever it may be. Any order which claims to be established without God is for him, disorder, whatever may be the apparent benefits that it promises. The only revolution is the one which consists in reforming what is contrary to the divine Law. At the same time this revolution seems to be an inescapable duty. It can concern man's salvation. It is within the frame of reference of his social, economic, and international relations that he must obey God, and if he does not, he sins. His relation with God, far from weakening his temporal obligation, makes it more implacable.

Now we must explain exactly what this obedience is. There is an obedience which leans on a false submission to divine providence, and which justifies any actual situation because it is an expression of God's will. This obedience is to the right as well as to the left. To the right, it is a justification of the established order which is seen as an expression of the divine law. To reverse this order would be a sacrilege. To the left, it is a justification of the revolution which is explained as the expression of an inescapable historical movement. Submission to this historical movement will assume something of a mystical character. It will justify every act. This is what Garaudy discloses in *Le communisme et la morale*. Men on the right will defend obedience as guarantee of what is; men on the left will claim that it is the guarantee of what will be.

But Christian obedience (because the Gospel assumes and stresses the doctrine of the

Old Testament) is precisely, not submission to the plain fact but to the *berith*, to the covenant. It is a perpetual correction of what is, according to what ought to be. Therefore it is absurd to identify the Gospel with any regime whatsoever — monarchy or democracy, liberalism or *dirigisme*. Each one of these regimes has its abuses. Christian obedience will not consist in accepting them blindly or clinging to them foolishly but in struggling to keep them subject to divine law. Christian obedience is thus seen to be the practice of liberty within human societies because it affirms that it is more important to obey God than to obey man. It is in the measure in which this dependence on God is made rigorous that man is guaranteed against oppression in the temporal cities.

* * *

The question is this. In a world which, even de-Christianized, remained penetrated with the values of Christianity, a certain respect for justice, law, and authority could prevail, although without theological roots, like the fragance of an empty perfume bottle. But those days are over. Now, origins have to be re-discovered because all the great ideas which have ceased to be connected with God are without foundation, justification or efficacy. Like shadows without any substance, they wander across our world, at the mercy of any one who wishes to exploit them. So we realize that their revolutionary value depended on their relation to God. To reestablish this relation to God seems to us to be essential today. This is problem number one.

Liberty

4

A characteristic trait of modern man is his awareness of the extent of his liberty. All movement of thought since the sixteenth century is towards the discovery of the subjective world. The human person was seen to transcend the whole objective world, whether this was the world of nature or the world of society. But this, in the end, led to a reversal of perspectives. Faced with creative liberty which, for a Sartre is totally unconditioned, and which dashes itself against a world in which there is no light, man has come to feel a kind of nausea. What is he to do with a liberty which is empty, without object, without end, knowing no law but its own? Liberty like this is a burden too heavy to bear. And so this explains — as Dostoievsky saw prophetically in *The Legend of the Great Inquisitor* — why men seek to free themselves from it at any cost. This explains the otherwise incomprehensible paradox of why men cling to communism, not in spite of the surrender it demands, but precisely because of it.

The shifting to and fro between two contradictory attitudes, between existentialism and communism, sometimes by the same individuals, clearly shows that there is a dichotomy in the way the problem is presented. It is true that the human person is greater than all private ends. But it is also true that it is necessary for him to be part of a whole. Therefore, the problem is to know where he really belongs. And it seems right that this must be in a position of dependence to a reality like himself but greater than he and which must necessarily be personal. It is only by submitting to God's plan that man can control his freedom without destroying it. Not only does man in this way not destroy his freedom but by the very act of submission he completely achieves it. Because — in spite of another illusion of modern thought — this freedom in which man glories is itself captive and must be freed. Thus submission to God, in which modern atheism sees an alienation, is on the contrary the fulfillment of freedom. This truth we would like to develop here more completely in the form that the problem presents itself today to some men — the problem of submission to the Church.

* * *

When the problem of the relation of Christianity and freedom is stated, it would seem at first that this means that adhesion to Christianity could not be a free act. As a matter of fact, the whole Christian tradition testifies to the price that

God attaches to human freedom. Gregory of Nyssa wrote : " To constrain man by force to accept the Gospel would have been contrary to his dignity because it is his freedom which makes him like God. " [1] Péguy echoes this same tradition when he writes : " The price of salvation is infinite, but what kind of salvation would there be that is not freely chosen? " [2] The only thing that has value in God's sight is a love that is free : " Once, a love that is freely given is known, supplications lose all their flavor. " [3]

The Christian's freedom in the approach to faith and in the practice of faith, is a preliminary question. But there is another aspect of the question which is its counterpart and which expresses the very heart of the Christian message, namely that faith is also the source of freedom. Here freedom has a new meaning. Here it is no longer man's nature inasmuch as he is a spirit and has the power of self-determination. But it is freedom in so far as it is the condition of a man freed from slavery. Now it must be said that this liberty is really the true question. Systems of philosophy and scientific advances have always tried to give man this freedom. Because of what value is it to will to be free, if one cannot be free? Against this wall crashes the freedom which modern existentialism has conceived. Man at every moment acts with self determination. But he is confronted by a world which he cannot understand and against which he is broken. He is his own master : he is not the master of the world.

[1] *Patr. Graec.*, 46, 524 A.   [2] *Œuvres Complètes*, p. 353.   [3] *Ibid.*, p. 354.

There will be wise men who will tell us that world mastery is unimportant, that man ought to give up willing what he cannot achieve, that true freedom is to be found in being free from all desire for what does not depend on us, and in being content with what we can control. They tell us that we must rule at least one kingdom, that is the kingdom of our own inner world. The man who wants nothing that depends on chance is inwardly free. Nothing can fetter him. He has entered into the free world. Nevertheless only a few wise men can win for themselves freedom of this kind. The great mass of men are prisoners of their own servitudes.

Others come forward to affirm that man ought and can free himself from these external servitudes. They acknowledge his present captivity. But man, they say, can escape. Through scientific advances, he will gradually triumph over biological enslavements, he will keep sickness at a distance and push back the frontiers of death. He will equate to will with to be able. Man's freedom will be man's own achievement. Prometheus will rise from the womb of a captive human race. He will triumph over economic enslavement, through the organization of the world. He will free man from exploitation by man. And the crowning achievement of this power will be a city of free men who will have won their own freedom.

Now Christianity denies all this. The freedom wise men offer is an illusion. Man may free himself from external servitudes, but if he examines himself he will discover his own internal servitudes, because man's inner freedom is itself held captive by a spiritual servitude which is far greater than material servitudes. Such inner freedom has not even the strength to will the true goods which are not the possession of its own self but which are the spiritual goods that God has reserved for those He loves. This inner freedom can be freed from the outer world but it is not freed from itself. It escapes from one captivity only to fall into another.

The freedom offered by technicians and politicians is also an illusion. It may modify in some way man's prison. It may make his prison a little bigger, and may enable him to live more comfortably. It does not take him out of his prison. It cannot take him out. Because if it pushes back the boundaries of biological existence, it still leaves man in a biological state. Life which it would make immortal, remains mortal life. And this immortalization of mortal life is worse than death. Because it is this mortal life which is in itself captivity, and it is only on the plane of another existence that freedom begins.

Now the Gospel affirms that there is only One who can deliver man from his captivity, the captivity of sin and the captivity of death, slavery to self or slavery to the world — and this is Jesus Christ. Jesus Christ alone descended into the depths of man's captivity, into the hells in which he is enclosed, in order to vanquish the power of death and sin, in order to break the prison's brazen bars which hold man captive. Jesus Christ's salvific action in the paschal mystery is man's liberation. The very word redemption means the freeing of a slave whom a master acquires in order to introduce him to the life of a free man. Christ redeemed captive mankind at the price of His own blood.

Thus with Christ is inaugurated a new creation freed from its servitudes. Only insofar as men are in Christ are they free. " For you have been called to liberty, brethren " (Gal. 5 : 13). Now this incorporation in Christ is made through faith and baptism. This means that faith leads to liberty : " But before the faith came we were kept imprisoned under the Law. . . . But now that faith has come, we are no longer under a tutor. For you are all the children of God through faith in Christ Jesus " (Gal. 3 : 23-26). Man, therefore, is no longer a slave of the external servitude of death : " You have risen with Christ " (Col. 3 : 1); and he is no longer a slave of the internal servitude of sin : " And having been set free from sin, you have become the slaves of justice " (Rom. 6 : 18).

Notice that Saint Paul adds that the Christian is also freed from the Law : " But when the fullness of time came, God sent His Son, born of a woman, born under the Law, that He might redeem those who were under the Law " (Gal. 4 : 4-5). This brings us to the positive aspect of spiritual freedom. This is not merely freedom from enslavements that are evil, it is also an entering into a new state, into the state of the sons of God. Now this is in a new sense an entering into freedom. As a result, man's relation to God is no longer that of a servant to a master, but that of a son to his Father. One alone is Son, He who is the only Son. It is in making us one with the only Son through the grace of filial adoption that faith and baptism lead us into the freedom of the sons of God.

Saint Paul used the word *parrhesia* to clarify the meaning of this kind of freedom. *Parrhesia* means freedom of speech. Among the Greeks it signified the condition of a citizen of the Athenian democracy who was able to speak freely in the assembly, that is in the *ecclesia*, to speak as a man among his equals, to speak without the fear of a subject in the presence of his master. Thus the gift of the Spirit which enables us to enjoy a mysterious participation in the divine nature gives us a right to this familiarity with the Father — a familiarity denied to the creature as such : " For whoever are led by the Spirit of God, they are the sons of God. Now you have not received a spirit of bondage so as to be again in fear, but you have received a spirit of adoption as sons, by virtue of which we cry, ' Abba! Father! ' " (Rom. 8 : 14-15).

Here it is not a question of a passage from evil to good but from a lower to a higher state, from the category of slave to that of friend. The Law was not bad, but it was provisional. It was meant to lead us to freedom. " The Law was established for those who were servants. It educated the soul by means of external things so that, advancing by way of obedience to precepts, man might learn to serve God. But at last the moment came when man had grown accustomed to the service of God and the bonds had to be broken so that this service could be freely given. " [1]

This brings us to a final aspect of freedom. Only where freedom is perfect does it tend of its own accord to the good, not because of a constraining law but because of the weight of love. Saint Thomas Aquinas has explained in a masterful way how freedom follows grace : " He is free, who is a cause unto himself. . . . The Holy Ghost then, rendering us lovers of God, inclines us to act of our own will, freely, out of love, not as bondsmen prompted by fear. . . . He takes away . . . that servitude whereby man acts according to the law, but against the motion of his will. " [1]

So, whether we love without or within, whether we consider man's power or his will, we never find freedom apart from grace. " For it is God who of His good pleasure works in you both the will and the performance. " (Phil. 2 : 13). Freedom begins in grace, if it is true that the very movement by which freedom moves towards faith is, according to Saint Augustine, made possible by grace. Freedom grows in grace, if the whole Christian existence is the process of the freeing of freedom by grace. Freedom attains its fullness in grace, if this fullness is the freedom of the sons of God and if the sons of God are those " who are led by the Spirit. "

Finally, this docility to the Spirit, which is spiritual freedom, is not the destruction but the realization of freedom inasmuch as this consists

[1] Iraeneus, *Adv. Haer.*   [2] *Summa Contra Gentiles*, IV, 22.

in the will's power of self-determination. Freedom does not consist in being able to do no matter what. It is the act of a will that turns spontaneously towards the good. Now it is the Spirit who inclines the will, under the pressure of love, to turn spontaneously towards the good. It is through Him that the movement of freedom is made one with the order of liberty. The problem is not how to discover a way to reconcile the work of freedom and the work of grace, as if it were a question of some kind of a compromise between the two; just as it is not an attempt to reconcile freedom and authority, as if it were a question of preventing trespassing from either side. The Christian takes the stand that grace is where freedom flourishes, just as the Church is where it is achieved. It is this aspect that suggests another question.

* * *

This is the question of the relation of spiritual freedom, as we have just defined it, and the authority of the Church. Today many may find the two incompatible. Has Saint Paul not written : " But the spiritual man judges all things, and he himself is judged by no man " (1 Cor. 2 : 15)? These words are interpreted to mean that man is directly inspired by the Spirit who frees souls from all institutional authority. This message of liberty should be found in the Gospel which contains the essence of the Christian message. But to acknowledge this is to become subject to the law. The Gospel, we are told, has unhappily been changed into the Church, the religion of the Spirit into the religion of authority. Men are willing to accept Christ but not the Church. More than this, they claim that to deny the Church is to be loyal to Christ. They declare they will brook no changes made in His message.

This opposition takes many shapes. It is characteristic of a certain form of liberal Protestantism, like that of Sabatier and Harnack, where we recognize the influence of German idealism. Traces are also found in Bergson's theory of opposed forces : static religion (that of an institution) versus dynamic religion (that of the spirit). In this light biblical authorities are sometimes examined and it is alleged that the continuing conflict between prophets and priests is a constant of religious history which reappears in early Christian days in the opposition between authority and charismatic gifts.

I shall offer only one example of this attitude, that of a Christian thinker who has praised freedom. For this reason his work seems excellent to me when his thought touches the problem of the Church. In his vindication of the absolute sovereignty of the subjectivity of the person, Berdiaev places the Church in what he calls the objective world. In his eyes, this always constitutes an alienation.

> There is a Church in the existential sense of the word, insofar as it is the realization of the communal spirit among men, and there are Churches which are but the externalization of simple social institutions. Idolatry and slavery begin when a Church, insofar as it is an

externalization and a social institution, is proclaimed holy and infallible. This is a deformation of religious life which is thereby invaded by a demoniacal power. [1]

In these lines we can recognize the profile of the Great Inquisitor, Dostoievsky's symbol of the Roman Church. But we can also see why many of our contemporaries, especially those who think along existentialist lines, equate the Roman Church with other forms of totalitarianism and why, in the name of freedom, they refuse to accept the Church.

There are many possible answers to all this. First of all, let us get rid of certain pseudo-historic charges, I mean the alleged opposition of prophets to priests, whether this be conceived as a movement against the Church or as movement within the Church. On the basis of the very latest exegetical knowledge, it must be said, that there does not seem to be any foundation whatsoever for this charge. There is no evidence in the Old Testament because the prophets, as Neher has recently shown in the case of Amos, never attacked the institutional hierarchy. On the contrary, they did all they could to serve the priesthood by bringing it back to its purity. [2] The same is true of early Christian beginnings as the protestant Oscar Cullmann has clearly shown in his study of the relation of charisms and the institution of the Church. [3] Looking at this question from another point of view, it must be said that although the

[1] *De l'esclavage et de la liberté de l'homme*, p. 279.
[2] *Amos*, p. 215.   [3] *Le Culte dans l'Eglise primitive*, p. 15 ff.

71

Spirit given in Baptism frees man from the Law, as Saint Paul teaches, nevertheless this liberty is given in an incomplete way. It is found in a man who is still a slave of the flesh. Saint Paul gives us an admirable description of the conflict of these two laws. " For the creature was made subject to vanity, not willingly, but by reason of him that made it subject, in hope. Because the creature also itself shall be delivered from the servitude of corruption, into the liberty of the glory of the children of God. For we know that every creature groaneth, and travaileth in pain, even till now. " (Rom. 8 : 20-22).

Thus liberty is not given at the beginning : it is a conquest. It exists only where my will, freed from its servitudes, can freely adhere to the good it loves. This is what Saint Augustine described in his *Confessions*. He shows the progressive liberation of love long held captive, whose chains grace shatters one by one. In this way he makes us understand that grace and liberty far from being opposed are functions of each other. It is grace that makes us free. Nevertheless the liberation of the spiritual man is the enslavement of the carnal man. Before the spiritual man in me loves the law of the Spirit as the very expression of my being, it is made subject in me by the carnal man whose wishes it constrains and denies.

In this way the authority of the Church will be the expression of this constraint which is the very path that leads to liberty. The implacable exigencies of the morality of the Church will be the means which will enable the man who is still carnal to free himself from the slavery of his passions, although the rigor of its dogmatic formulas will first seem constraining to the intellect that does not adhere to them with joyous enthusiasm. The pedagogical role of the Law in the training of mankind in the Old Testament is found again in the spiritual itinerary of every man to the good and the true so that one day he can freely embrace them.

But were we to go no further it might seem that the authority of the Church were but a provisional stage, necessary to a still frail freedom, but from which the truly spiritual man would be freed. That is why we must go on to say that the bond of the Church is more profound than this and it constitutes a permanent factor. This is exactly what Berdiaev challenged because he was wrong on two counts, on the nature of the Church, and on the nature of spiritual freedom. And because this double error is the reason why many men today refuse to accept the Church, we must examine the subject.

The basis for such an attitude is a confusion about the true nature of the Church. Berdiaev wrote : " It is impossible to speak of the Church as of higher unity and one that is exterior, one that is a Whole. To speak of the Church as of an organism is to use a biological analogy that cannot be carried very far. " The relation of the Church to its members would in this way become the primacy of the totality over the individuals. It is true that Saint Paul says that the Church is the Body of Christ and that Christians are the members of this Body. It is also true that this figure has, in our day, been understood in a biological sense. Under Hegel's influence, Moehler did this to a certain extent in *The Unity of the Church*. The Tübingen school has not always been free from this conception. But it must be added that the encyclical *Mystici corporis* was directed precisely against this idea, which was stigmatized as the corruption of ecclesiology by sociology. The unity of the Church is not the primacy of the collectivity above persons but the bond which unites the members inasmuch as they have the same head, Christ. [1]

Furthermore, when Berdiaev speaks of spiritual freedom, the expression may cause confusion because he uses it to designate the person in his transcendence in relation to things. It is this subjectivity of the person which he will not allow to be made subordinate to any objective world. This total freedom is based on the spiritual nature of the person. But here the word spiritual is used equivocally. To Berdiaev it means that man's very nature is spirit. And this spirit is liberty. To us this nature remains captive as long as man is left to himself. It must be freed through the power of the Holy Spirit. Spiritual liberty is the freedom of the created spirit when, through the Holy Spirit, it is freed from the slavery of sin.

Only through the Holy Spirit then is spiritual liberty given. But it must be added, on the other hand, that it is only in the Church that the power of the Holy Spirit is at work. In fact

[1] Cf. Louis BOUYER, "Où en est la Théologie du Corps Mystique," *Rev. Sciences Religieuses*, 82, May 1948, p. 318 ff.

it is to the Church, His spouse, that Christ has given His Spirit. And this Church is not "the existential center of the ecumenical conscience" of which Berdiaev spoke. It is a visible Church to which Christ has bound His Spirit so that it is by contact with the visible magisterium of this Church that the intellect is enlightened by this Spirit, and by contact with the visible sacraments of this Church that the soul receives life from Him.

Thus the Church is not opposed to spiritual liberty but is its source. It is the Spirit who is the bond between the Church and liberty. In fact, for the Christian, two propositions are certain : freedom is bound to the Spirit and the Spirit is bound to the Church. Man seeks freedom and so he turns to the Spirit. Man then seeks the Spirit and therefore goes to the Church. Saint Paul spoke correctly when he said that " the spiritual man judges all things, and he himself is judged by no man " (1 Cor. 2 : 15). But this man is spiritual only insofar as he is united with the Church. To be able to judge all things, he must first of all be judged by the Church from whom he receives the Spirit by whom he can judge all things.

*
* *

But is the Church who frees us also free? This is the adversaries' last stand. It is true that the powers of darkness roam about seeking whom they may devour as they once circled about Christ. But the presence of the Spirit in the Church reveals itself precisely by that sovereign freedom which is hers despite so many snares. Of this the best proofs are the persecutions of which the Church is the object, as well as the efforts men make to corrupt her. These prove that in a world enslaved, the Church stands as the refuge of freedom. This is why the powers which seek to devour mankind fling themselves against the Church with such violence. If the Church is the homeland of men who are free it is first of all because it is itself free in respect to everything that is not the inner bond of love.

Certitude

5

The problem of faith confronts man today more totally than ever before. It is a question, not so much of specific difficulties, such as the historicity of Christ or the existence of evil, but of the value of the religious attitude itself. Atheism, once the belief of a few individuals and a term of reprobation, now is held far more widely and enjoys a certain prestige. In this chapter I wish to examine contemporary intellectual attitudes that present a preliminary obstacle to the possibility of faith by discrediting the position it represents. Perhaps a closer examination will disclose the fact that these prejudices are less forceful than they seem at first.

* * *

One set of difficulties belongs to the strictly intellectual order. The modern mind is to a large extent formed by the positive methods of

79

the physical sciences and mathematics. For this reason man today is accustomed to criteria of certitude that belong to this domain. This is true not only of the scholar, strictly so called, but of many men who believe that scientific methods are the norm of all truth. These men are all at ease when they are presented with facts of faith and motives of credibility. They feel that their usual criteria cannot be applied here. And this is true in two ways. On the human plane, dogmatic facts which are the object of faith, whether they be the creation of man or the resurrection of Christ, have been transmitted to us by testimony, like every historical reality. To a scientific mind this order of reality never seems to reach anything higher than approximate certitude and lacks the rigor of the exact sciences.

Moreover, the facts of revelation come from a realm inaccessible to human reason. They deal with the intimate life of God and the gratuitous participation in this life given to man by Jesus Christ. Therefore, unlike mathematical propositions and physical laws, they cannot be proved on intrinsic evidence; for the formal motive of faith is to be found, not in the object known, since it is unknowable by definition, but in the veracity of the one who makes it known. This is the testimony of Scripture, it is eminently that of Christ, and in its continuity that of the Church — and it is the reason why the believer accepts revealed truths. Now this acceptance of a truth for which he has no evidence leaves the mind of the modern man uneasy; he questions the honesty of an act that implies a kind of surrender.

This does not mean that he denies the value of faith in itself but that he despairs of finding for it a communicable justification. Faith is recognized as a personal experience which carries with it its own evidence yet is incapable of being objectively established. It is remarkable how often this attitude is to be found among scientifically trained men. They feel a certain fear whenever there is any discussion of the reasons for their belief, just as if they were afraid that the discussion might lead to reason for doubt. They make a sharp distinction between intellectual operations, where they admit no laws except those of the positive disciplines, and acts of the spiritual life which are based on religious sentiment and express a strictly personal experience.

The dangers of this form of fideism are obvious. There is a failure to distinguish between the domain of religious sentiment and that of the assent of faith. Admittedly the meeting of the soul with God is always a personal encounter and in this sense is incommunicable. But this encounter is not conditioned by temperament or type of mind. It is within the competence of every human being. Some men are rigorously positive and are unsuited to mystical speculations but are capable of becoming admirable believers. Others are religiously inclined and can easily be misled by the most doubtful ideologies. Faith is offered to all. It is the acceptance of the message of Christ and the Church. My problem is not to discover whether this message suits me but whether it is valid in itself. If it is valid then I must accept it, even if my mind or sensibilities resist it on other grounds.

In the same way, if the act of faith opens man's mind to transcendent reality, it is still true to say with Pascal that " Nothing is more reasonable than this disavowal of reason. " Surely the signs by which the living God manifests Himself to a soul may be of many kinds but it is true that although this acceptance may be beyond reason it is never contrary to reason. The Church has always insisted on the " rational justification of faith. " This is not, as a certain type of fideism would have it, a leap into the absurd to escape from the prison of evidence, but it is a higher certitude that is consistent with the certitudes of reason.

This is true of the approach to faith. Granted this is not the conclusion of a rational demonstration. The motives of a conversion are not necessarily the most cogent but those that make possible the soul's meeting with God. Yet this acceptance must meet the tests of rational criticism which will show that faith's foundations are solid and that faith's justification is not some emotional outburst but a tried and stable reality. This involves metaphysical truths. The whole Christian tradition testifies to the accord between philosophy and theology. This also involves historic truths. For three centuries critics have tried in every way to disprove the traditional facts or events connected with revelation which stand today more secure than ever before.

Reason's role is not limited to the preambles of faith. It continues to function within the very act of faith where its work is one of purification. It distinguishes authentic and enlightened faith from its caricatures which are known as illuminism, fanaticism, obscurantism. True faith does not fear philosophical speculations or the progress of science. These may present new problems which at first are disconcerting. But efforts to meet these problems cleanse faith from much that was transitory and contingent. They force the theologian not to confuse faith with its restricted teachings of cosmology or psychology. Were he to refuse to make these efforts he would sin by laziness and add to the scandal of the cross, which must always be a faulty presentation for which he alone is responsible.

So we conclude that it is a deformation of the modern mind that leads to the defeatism of many of our contemporaries who are unable to accept the support that reason can bring to faith and forces them to turn to purely subjective criteria because they admit no certitude but that of the positive sciences. This is to deny that the human mind is capable of attaining other truths than those that are the result of experimentation and scientific conclusions. Not only is this a certitude without privilege but its world, which is that of matter, is also a world in which reality is most relative.

Metaphysical certitude and historical certitude, far from belonging to some measure of incertitude, are themselves primary. The crisis we are here analyzing seems at first to be a metaphysical crisis. Even though some will not go so far as to say with a Karl Barth that certitude is essentially a sacriligeous pretention of human reason, they do insist that it is impossible to attain certitude. Is it not one of the duties of our day to reestablish confidence in the intellect which is made to contemplate truth and which faith strengthens in the natural order and raises to the supernatural order.

Certitude in the historical order is based on knowledge acquired by testimony. This disquiets a mind trained in the positive sciences. Yet this disquiet has no foundation. Jean Guitton has shown that testimony is the foundation on which rest the basic values of human life. And testimony can afford a certitude that is just as rigorous as any other. To continue to question this certitude, indicates an inability to trust and a deeply rooted doubt from which some minds suffer as from an illness — unless it be the expression of a subtle pride which accepts only such truths as it can grasp and fears the dispossession of self that faith brings.

* * *

Thus the first set of difficulties may be traced to an attitude of mind that has been shaped by modern civilization. But there are other and deeper difficulties. More serious are those that spring from what seems most precious to man today : courage, sincerity, lucidity. Granted, it will be said, the truths proposed by Christianity are admirable. They provide solutions to problems every man must face. These solutions correspond to his most profound wishes. Yet it is this that most disturbs us. Is there not the danger that a man believes because he wishes to believe? Is there not the risk that the judgment is influenced by what he desires? Faith has many accomplices within us : the desire of sharing beliefs dear to those around us, the consolation that religion can bring. . . . All this constitutes a force to which it is difficult not to yield.

If we look at faith in this light it becomes the expression of a weakness, a need for support, a refuge. Surely it will not be denied that there is some truth in all this. Souls in need of the consolations of religion should not be deprived of them for it must be admitted that they can be of great value. But the clear-headed man must have the courage to do without them, to face reality even if this brings only sadness. Paradoxically, it is the very beauty of Christianity that alienates certain souls today. It seems too beautiful to be true. It offers too easy a solution to the problems with which they struggle. They fear that acceptance would mean a descent. They harden themselves against it in the name of what they consider to be best in themselves : their honesty and their intellectual courage.

Faith is understood to be a consolation for the heart, a comfort for the mind, a refuge to which men turn in order to escape from the hard fate of ceaselessly confronting an unknown world, having no other resources than those afforded by the human intelligence :

> Philosophy is the continual awareness, conti-
> nually renewed, that can take place only in

the instant. What troubles me a little in supernatural knowledge is its slightly bourgeois character; it is the comfortable settling down in something permanent and stable. [1]

Faith seems to be a premature anticipation in which man goes beyond the evidence of his personal experience and which does not ring true. More modest and more immediately realizable claims would be preferable.

If a little while ago we were thinking of a positivistic type of mind, now we are alluding to a form of contemporary humanism, the humanism of a Camus, a Malraux a Thierry Maulnier. There is a certain fascination about their attitude. But is this the attitude of the true believer? The reluctance of those men would be justified by the terms we have just used. But do these terms really represent the tenets of the true believer? First of all, is the attitude of faith so easy? It is true that a certain apologetic presents it as satisfying my longings for happiness in a way no finite object ever could. I realize that such a presentation, even if it is partly true, has about it something suspect. Might faith not be but the projection of my desires? As a matter of fact it is in reality utterly different. The reality of God is present to me in the measure in which He is someone who resists me, whom I cannot change, against whom I struggle. He resists my will in the absolute of good and evil. He resists my intelligence in the apparent arbitrariness of His interventions. And if I am aware of Him it

[1] V. JANKELEVITCH, *La connaissance de l'homme au XXe siècle*, p. 310.

is because He contradicts my projects rather than favors them.

To accept God, therefore, is to accept the irruption into my life of a presence that will never again leave me quiet. Jacques Rivière spoke of " love and its immense disturbances. " To accept God, to accept His love, means to be willing to be always disturbed, in my longing for self-satisfaction, in my desire for self-possession. It means to be willing never again to be my own but always to be at the mercy of another. If the unbeliever is sincere, will he not admit that in reality what keeps him far from the faith is less the comfort he fears to find there than the dread that once he has placed a finger on the button he will be carried further than he wishes to go? He has a presentiment that faith will endanger his desire for independence, autonomy of judgement, personal freedom. He shrinks from this dispossession, this poverty. Let him not hide his fear of love's adventures behind a hypocritical diffidence about faith's alleged comforts.

But, it will be objected, even if faith entails serious obligations, it must be admitted that it also brings with it a definitive solution to man's problems and puts an end to his searching and disquiet. Once again, it must be asserted that the unbeliever has oversimplified the picture. In reality, man does not believe because all his problems are resolved, but because his problems are not resolved. Some seekers after faith erroneously believe that the search ends after all objections have been answered. A Christian is not a man whose objections have vanished. Certainly faith brings light for many problems. But it often happens that on the rational plane the Christian has as many difficulties as the unbeliever. The only difference is that, in spite of the difficulties, he believes, basing his belief in God's testimony.

This also shows that faith puts no end to the search. This continues untouched in all domains unconnected with faith. In the scientific world there is no difference between the believer and the unbeliever and faith places no limits here to freedom of research. In philosophical problems, such as evil or liberty, surely faith provides the Christian with elements of the solution but he will never cease trying to formulate answers because the limitations of his mind remain the limitations of all minds. Here he must share the research of the unbeliever. Faith, far from limiting his research, opens new fields, for the new realities to which it introduces the believer are full of mystery. The mind enlightened by grace tries to understand them without ever being able to exhaust them. According to the old saying, faith seeks to understand, *fides quaerens intellectum*. In this there is nothing of the immobility of a mind faced with no problems and needing only repose.

Therefore research continues within faith inasmuch as there are problems that remain unresolved for me. But these problems are resolved in themselves and I can rest on this certitude. Faith is this rest. It is precisely this (if we go to the bottom of the subject) that is repugnant to modern minds. They do not want to acknowledge that the act of intelligence consists in adhering to an anterior reality, for this implies submission and dependence. The exercise of intelligence has savor for them only insofar as it is creative and inventive. The restlessness they insist on is man's affirmation of his pure contingence. It is an election of becoming rather than of being, of the contingent rather than of the absolute; it is the denial of God.

So we see that what appeared first as a fear of intellectual comfort is once again a refusal of dependence, a willed absolute autonomy. To acknowledge that essence precedes existence, God precedes man, is to acknowledge that I do not dispose of myself, that I must enter an order that I have not invented.

It is just this that some minds will not accept. Yet this is a basic option since it concerns the essence of the religious attitude which is to acknowledge that I do not stand alone but that I receive myself from another. Contemporary humanism refuses this dependence. It flees from truth as from a prison. It tries to build its artificial paradises on truth's borders where at last it can find a home. But it succeeds only in enclosing itself in an absurd solitude where the only human act becomes revolt and refusal.

Finally, and this is the last objection, it is claimed that in adhering to faith's affirmations one must anticipate one's self. In the Christian there is necessarily a wide margin between what he affirms and what he is. Is this not to condemn him to live in the unauthentic? Certainly it is true that this discrepancy between the affirmations of the Gospel and the reality of the Christian world is painful. But does authenticity consist here in equating affirmations and realizations, or in testifying to a truth even when it condemns you? Pharisaism consists in the will to be right, in the claim to be just, and establishing one's own norms of justice. Christian sincerity consists in acknowledging this inauthenticity which is man's sinful being. It is this humility that leads to truth and is true sincerity.

* * *

At the present moment there is a third and final set of difficulties. Contemporary man is above all else concerned with action and efficiency. Because of his great needs and opportunities, his aim is to bring about an improvement in the temporal order through the use of all the forces that modern technics and organization place at his command. Religious life seen in this perspective seems to orient towards God's world human energies needed here below. This can lead to a simple practical denial of religion, for which men can now find no time, absorbed as they are by their temporal duties.

This attitude can be expressed in a theory such as we see in Marxism. Religion is presented as a projection in a metaphysical heaven by mankind frustrated in this present life because of false economic conditions. It is a sublimation, a derivative of man's vital forces, an opiate. Atheistic humanism would escape from this magic by explaining the mists of mystification with which it is surrounded. It does all it can to restore to man his essence which he has projected and alienated in God. In this way man recovers all his strength to conquer in his own way the only paradise he is able to reach and which he must create for himself. Man becomes man's demiurge through the transformation of the conditions of his existence.

Of course under this dogmatic form, atheistic humanism is rejected by many minds. But the mere fact of concentrating all one's strength on the temporal combat may force even Christians to relegate to second place purely religious activities such as adoration, contemplation, penance. Religious life will be gradually emptied of its reality and reduced to practical formulae. The temptation might be to abandon an apparently purposeless faith which had been allowed to be deprived of its substance. Now this often supposes at the beginning the acceptance of a concept of faith which was nothing more than a solution to personal problems and which failed to see that God's plan, which is its object, embraces the total destiny of mankind and the world.

It must be admitted that if such an idea has become widespread, Christians are in part responsible. First of all on the theoretical plane, the charge of idealism that Marx levels against religion in general and Christianity in particular, is only apparently true. Christians seem to be indifferent to the material world and its transformations. Today man grapples with matter. He is delighted and pleased with its potentialities.

A doctrine ignoring all the things that fill his life will seem strange and abstract. On the practical plane, too, Christians often allow their faith to be divorced from their profane activities. They are now reproached for this divorce. Today man's attention is concentrated on profane activities which seem to satisfy him and separate him from God.

As a matter of fact, living faith far from being an evasion demands action. It is concerned with the betterment of temporal society. It requires the Christian layman to find ways of ensuring justice, of providing workers with conditions to which they are entitled. Faith and action are not two separate domains. But faith gives the Christian a motive for action all the stronger because of obedience to a divine law. In this way what is given to God is not taken from man. Love of God and love of man are not two opposing magnitudes and, if Christians have neglected their temporal obligations, it is not because they have loved God too much. It is absurd to say that faith withdraws man from his duties to the world.

The Christian's service of his neighbor cannot be limited to meeting temporal needs. His realism embraces the whole man. He knows that if there are corporal miseries, there are also spiritual miseries. He knows that man is a citizen not only of the city on earth but also of the city of God. He knows that this material world is part of God's creation and will one day be transfigured. Faith offers a vision of the world that embraces all things in the perspective of God's plan. God is at work in our midst, we are impelled to be His co-workers. True achievement involves man in work which transcends the limits of the earthly city and opens into eternity.

Therefore modern man, engaged in work, does not find faith difficult because he fears it will take him away from his work. He finds it difficult, and this must be recognized at once, because our world with its relations between religious life and temporal society presents extremely complex problems for which the findings of sociology are indeed impressive. Many of these problems are linked with actual situations and with historic facts, each one of which constitutes a special case. More radically the difficulty can be traced to the temptation, peculiar to modern man, to be self-sufficient and to depend on no one. Here the difficulty will be all the greater because it is collective in form, as a temptation of all mankind, and thus it will seem to be the disinterested service of an ideal. It will also seem to be the expression of the very means of power that man has created for himself and which has given him unlimited confidence in his own possibilities.

* * *

To conclude: difficulties against faith are shared by believer and non-believer. They are not to each other as he who possesses is to he who is to receive. For this reason the believer can remain humble and not be right in such a way, as Maritain once observed, that will make others want to adopt the opposite point of view. The man who believes is a man, who in spite of the difficulties of his intellect, in spite of the repugnance of his will, thinks that the word of Jesus Christ merits the full support of his whole intellect and his whole will. When Christ first proposed to those about Him the doctrine of the Eucharist they found it hard to accept. The greater number withdrew. But Peter, in the name of a few faithful souls, gave the answer which we make our own: " Lord, to whom shall we go? You have the words of eternal life. "

Faith

6

Many Catholics today have a surface religion consisting of such practices as Sunday Mass, Friday abstinence and Easter duties, and which is linked with family traditions, social customs and sentimental associations. It never occurs to them that the Gospel exacts anything more. Consequently they willingly accuse themselves in their annual confession of missing Mass on Sunday, of eating meat on Friday, but were the confessor to inquire whether they had failed against charity, they would feel affronted. Nor can they long resist the sociological pressure of the modern world when relations are close and the individual must act as an individual. Rightly, therefore, is Catholicism of this caliber challenged today by many men who hold that religion must be the result of personal convictions.

But this reaction against a Catholicism of purely external practice, in itself legitimate and salutary, tends to minimize the value of the Church's external practices and the need of a visible expression of faith. Some go still further and, discounting the value of Mass and the Sacraments, try to reduce Catholicism to an ethic of brotherly love and philanthropy. They attack not only the empty formalism of some believers but the whole visible, sacramental and liturgical aspect of the Church. The cause of their attack is a serious deviation which can be corrected by a statement of the true meaning of the sacramental life of the Church and an explanation of its absolute necessity and perfect legitimacy.

* * *

A letter received after a recent television appearance touches the heart of this question. It came from a young Catholic student and is so characteristic that it deserves exact quotation :

> Do you not think that a person who does not have the faith, but who leads a blameless life and devotes himself whole-heartedly to social good works has more chance of being saved than does a person who is baptized, but who leads a mediocre and selfish life, fulfilling the minimum obligations of a Catholic life, such as Mass on Sunday . . .? I am personally convinced that God, the Father of the Communist as well as of the Christian, will have at least as much place in His heaven for the man who lives a genuine life without knowing about Christianity as He will for the selfish and negligent Christian.

I shall now pause to examine an attitude which is quite common. Some seem to take for granted that the Communist is devoted and the Catholic is selfish. No doubt my correspondent would not go this far, but it is easy to detect a severity of judgement towards Catholics and a spontaneous sympathy towards others that seems resentful rather than objective. Proof of this can be found by questioning Catholics who live in a working man's milieu — I have in mind what Michelle Aumont has said — and they will tell you that there is in every worker a willingness to help one another, but that there is a depth of charity, a willingness to forgive, a disinterested love that are the fruit of the Gospel and are to be found only where God's grace has widened the narrowness of the human heart and given it the dimensions of Christ's love.

But this is a minor point. The essential characteristic in the statement quoted is the idea that the spirit of human brotherhood suffices to make a man a Catholic and son of God even if he does not believe in God. It is perfectly true that love of one's neighbor is the touchstone of the true love of God. Saint Augustine never tires repeating this. But it is equally true that the love of one's neighbor does not exempt one from the love of God. Rather, of the two commandments, it is the love of God which beyond any doubt is first. Catholicism is a religion before it is an ethic. The idea that a man can be a Catholic without first being religious is an aberration of the modern mind which empties Catholicism of its essence.

99

The essence of Catholicism, in so far as it is primarily a religion, consists in man's acknowledgment of his dependence on God. Any attitude that gives man an absolute value is completely anti-Christian. Let it not be said that concern for others suffices to make a man a Catholic. In fact modern idolatry has taken the form of an affirmation that man does not need God's help to love his fellowmen. Claudel has expressed this admirably : " Modern man is tempted to show that he can do good without God. " We are obliged today to go beyond the over-simplified equation : selfishness = anti-Christianism, altruism = Christianity.

Moreover, the acceptance of a Christianity which would replace God with man is not only anti-Christian, it is anti-human. The relationship of man to God is as constitutive of the human being as the relation of man to men. A man who does not pray is not a man. He lacks something essential. He is in part mutilated. Baudelaire once declared that the mark of a mediocre mind is to remain untouched by the divine grandeur. Adoration, the power of recognizing these grandeurs is always the sign of an eminent mind. This is the reason why in its relentless defense of religious values, Catholics are saving modern man from suffocation. This is the reason why a Catholic can never admit that a man who does not believe is a Catholic.

It is in this perspective that the value of religious practice, even in its most elementary forms, is seen. For it signifies in lives which are weak in other ways, a certain will to remain in contact with God. On this level religious practice is not something specifically Catholic but rather a human need. Men have always felt the need of making the essential acts of life sacred to God; for it is these acts which bring them, no matter how mediocre, to the frontier of mystery: the birth of a child, the union of man and wife, the meeting with death. They make openings, in even the most narrowly selfish existence, through which may shine a ray of creative and redemptive Love. I shall not praise the Catholic who has reduced his religion to a few religious acts. Nor shall I cast a stone. For in him I respect the smoldering flax, the reed that may grow straight again. When this little flame is nearly quenched, we will find ourselves in a world of darkness and of spiritual death, of civil marriages and state funerals. We will be in a world where there is dedication to humanity, progress and science, but where this dedication immolates men's lives to the monstrous idol which is their collective pride.

I understand what prompted the young student to write to me. She is right in suffering when Christians are so unchristian in their lives. She is right in thinking that an unbeliever may be obscurely inspired by a desire for God when he devotes himself to his fellowmen. We do not know the secrets of the heart and we do know that " God is greater than our heart, " according to the words of St. John that Mauriac quoted to Colette. But it remains objectively true that a man without God is without spiritual life. I fear that we may shape our theology to suit our desires.

It is not necessary to be a Christian to pity bodily pain. It suffices to be a man. But only a Christian can pity the far worse miseries of a soul, for they involve final and essential realities of existence.

[*]

So far we have remained on what we may call a pre-Christian level, and have discussed external rites in so far as they express religion in the broadest sense of the word. Sacraments represent an entirely different reality. They are so linked with the very essence of Catholicism that it is impossible to be a Catholic without sharing in them. Yet many question their necessity and significance. They ask if the sacraments are not part of some collective, exterior form of religion which seems of secondary importance. They gladly contrast a Christianity " in spirit and in truth " to a Christianity of rites and observances.

This discontent may have several causes. Their study will enable us to understand better the meaning of the sacramental system. One attitude would contrast interior Christianity and social religion. It can cite illustrious authorities. Henri Bergson in *Two Sources of Morality and Religion* opposes a closed religion which is the expression of the pressure of the collectivity on the individual, to a religion which is the expression of a personal inspiration uniting the soul to the *élan* of creative Love. The analyses of Durkheim provide the foundation for this study. Bergson was correct in refusing to explain religion in sociological terms. But he failed to realize that membership in a community is just as essential to man as personal existence. Furthermore the ecclesiastical institution instituted by Christ is in no way comparable to a collective organization, but is the divine establishment of an institutional structure to which Christ entrusted His message for the world.

In fact men today hold two equally false opinions about a visible Church. Some men, aware of the impulse that Mussolini called "the intoxication of collective life" which drives individuals to exultant fusion in a crowd, transpose this fusion into Catholicism and exaggerate its communal aspects at the expense of a personal life of prayer and asceticism. The liturgical movement, admirable though it be, can lead to dangerous deformities like this, if it is cultivated only along one line. The Catholic community is a community of persons and not a dissolution into an impersonal unity. It is worth what its members are worth. From a community of mediocre men will come only mediocrity.

Other men, realizing that personal values are imperiled wherever individuals through violence or persuasion, seek to lose themselves in a crowd, conceive such a horror of all collectivity that their view of the social side of Catholicism is affected. Simone Weil was typical of this group when she spoke with loathing of "the great beast." And it must be admitted that certain exaggerations of the doctrine of the Mystical Body, which turn it into a vague baptized collectivity, justify these attacks.

The correct view of the Church has little in common with these two attitudes. The institutional Church is the expression of God's will, according to which it is through a people, a community, that God communicates Himself to man. This is true of the Old Testament. Yahweh lives in the Tabernacle in the midst of the people of Israel. This is even more true of the Church, the bride of Christ, always holy, infallible, immaculate; to whom the Word her Spouse has given all that is His. This the Church, and the Church alone possesses, not by any right of nature but by a real and definitive gift. For it is from the Church that we receive the riches entrusted to her by Christ. Man seeks God. And we say to him : God is here, His power is operative, His word can be heard in the Church, His Tabernacle made of living stones.

The Sacraments are the actions by which we come in contact with the Church. They have a social character, as Father de Lubac has said in *Catholicism*. Baptism incorporates us into the ecclesiastical community and this incorporation enables us to share in the life of Christ. Penance, through the priest delegated for the office, reconciles us with the ecclesiastical community and with Christ. The Eucharist is the very expression of membership in the ecclesiastical community. It is in the midst of this community, united in His Name, that the Christ of glory makes Himself present. Marriage establishes husband and wife in their proper vocation of building up the Body of Christ.

On this basis it may be conceded that Catholicism implies a community. But, it may further be objected, why need the community express itself by exterior acts? Why should God think it important that we go to Mass on Sunday rather than Thursday? Or, that we assemble in one place to pray, rather than remain at home? After all, it is the interior disposition that counts in God's sight. Does not Isaias quote God as saying : " What need have I of the blood of he-goats and heifers? " It is not interior religion that alone matters? What does the external action add? Is there not the danger that this exterior action will satisfy us and we will fall into formalism and pharisaism?

A whole school of thought tries to justify these charges by saying that visible worship is necessary for simple folk but the elite may practice only interior worship which is the true religion. Long ago Origen said that " the masses need feasts. " Spinoza in his *Theological-Political Treatise* contrasted exterior worship, a necessity for the masses, to religion in spirit, which alone engages " philosophers. " Certainly as H. Duméry remarks this is not a final condemnation of visible worship but it does seem to relegate it to an inferior position.

Such a statement betrays a subtle pride. Visible worship is deemed a mere concession. Superior men need no such support. Does this attitude correspond to the Gospels? Do they not affirm that it is not human aptitudes, even religious aptitudes, that count? All men are sinners and all need God's grace whether they be learned or ignorant. Indeed, the wisdom of this world, insofar as it leads to pride is an obstacle to the humility of faith that refuses to recognize the littleness of the humble of this world. " The intelligent " and " the wise " reject the humble actions of the Sacraments but by so doing they shut themselves off from God who reveals Himself to the humble and lowly.

But there is something even more important. The Incarnation of God in humanity is of the essence of Catholicism. This is already true of Christ. He is the Word made flesh. It is by contact with His sensible humanity that men who live close to Him have access to His invisible divinity. Now the Church is the continuation of the Incarnation. She also is body and soul. She contains the divine mystery under humble appearances. It is only by contact with this visible appearance, with her body, with her visible structure, with her sacraments, that man can have access to the divine riches that are hers. Those who despise her because of the humility of her body, will deprive themselves forever of the riches of her Spirit.

We are now touching the essence of the Sacraments. They are sensible signs that produce invisible grace. Lowly water poured upon the forehead brings to the soul the life of the Spirit, a font bubbling with eternal life. Christ Himself is already a Sacrament. He meets man in His humanity, distributing bread, changing water into wine, and He leads man to His divinity. He makes Himself man to make us gods. So the sacraments, making use of the humble realities of our daily life, charge them with a mysterious content. Through them and by them we attain the riches of grace. The supernatural becomes flesh, as Péguy says. For the Word of God comes to take the whole man, body and soul to vivify him entirely by His Holy Spirit. Nothing is more contrary to this realism of the Holy Spirit than a form of spiritualism that disparages the flesh.

We come now to the last question. Some will ask : Is it not more important to perform an act of charity than to go to Mass? To fight for peace or better housing than to participate in a liturgical conference? We feel the breath of the Father of Lies on our face. We think of Sundays of socialist realism, sinister Sundays of a world without God, on which the construction of the city of men is substituted for the construction of the City of God.

This is the heart of the problem. There is a city of men to be constructed. There is good in what man creates, in what gives man glory. But there is also the City of God to be constructed. Far better is what God creates, what gives Him glory. The construction of the City of God is sacred history, the only real and lasting history. It is the history of the works of God to which the Old Testament gives witness. It is the history that culminates in the mysteries of Christ. The sacraments are the continuation in our midst of the divine action. We are living in the midst of sacred history. In our midst God lives, saves, makes an alliance, creates. And these works of God are greater than the works of man. To believe, is to believe this. We admire the works of man, but we admire more the works of God. Pascal said, " Jesus Christ invented nothing but He was holy, holy, holy, holy to God, terrible to the demon. " It is pitiful to find Catholics today who allow themselves to be so dazzled by the great deeds of men that they overlook the incomparably superiority of the grandeur of God.

Herein appears the true meaning of the Sacraments. They are the divine actions of Christ glorious living in His Church. Baptism and the Eucharist are the water and blood flowing until the end of time from the pierced side of the New Adam to give life to the world. In a magnificent vision the Apocalypse shows us the Holy Spirit as a river of living water flowing from the throne of God and of the Lamb, moving through the city which is the Church to make the trees of life flower in the new Paradise. So at the heart of the world the sacramental system represents this divinizing action, this vital milieu where begins eternal life which will one day pass beyond the barrier of death.

* * *

Return now to our starting point. We find that some would place Catholicism's external worship in opposition to fraternal charity and seek to extol the latter at the expense of the former — a highly doubtful procedure. The service of God is as basic an obligation as the service of our neighbor. Both demands are equally rigorous. A Catholic who minimizes either deceives himself. There is no world worthy of the name where both are not respected. A world without adoration is as inhuman as would be a world without brotherly love. La Pira says that in the true city, God and man, each has a home.

But to judge the sacraments on this level is still to touch only the surface of the problem. For the sacraments are much more. They are the means by which God's life springs up in the world and communicates to it incorruptibility. Catholicism is not merely the combination of a form of worship and ethics. It is the life of God calling into being the life of man. It is God coming in search of man. God always takes the initiative. That is why the origin of all Catholic life is an entering into the life of God. It is the sacraments that effect this. The principle of all Catholicism is the act of humility by which man, recognizing his radical inability to save himself, comes to ask the Church for the salvation God has given her to dispense. Outside the Church, outside the sacraments, there is no salvation. This is inexorably true. If there are men, as we are sure, who will be saved without belonging visibly to the Church, they are saved only because they have benefitted mysteriously from the superabundant grace of the visible Church. But they will not be saved either by their own virtues or their own learning. They will be saved in the measure that, one day, from the depths of their spiritual misery, they will have uttered a cry for help, making in this way an opening through which grace can enter in. Theologians call this baptism of desire.

But if it is clear that there is no Catholicism without sacraments, it is also clear that sacraments alone do not make the perfect Catholic. The reception of the sacraments is the first condition, without which there is not true Catholicism. This is the reason why any diminution in their reception is always a grave warning and why we must do all we can to prevent any diminution. But it is only the starting point. And if infidelity to the sacraments condemns some men, frequent reception justifies only those who allow the sacraments to bear fruit in their lives.

Hope

7

The problem of civilization's future cannot be evaded. This is an age of crisis. Events are of global consequence : technical inventions place in men's hands power never known before; economic upheavals shatter so-called classic economic laws and demand a re-examination of the distribution of wealth; lands across the sea, once held as colonies or kept economically dependent on the nations of the west, have won political autonomy.

The future fills some men with dread. All they hold dear seems in danger. They have never distinguished between eternal values and the expression of these values in terms of bourgeois civilization, therefore they feel that they must defend the past from the assaults of the future. Others, on the contrary, trust the new forces unreservedly and believe that scientific progress and social transformations will produce an earthly paradise.

We must ask ourselves what connection there is between Christian hope which has for its object the heavenly city, and temporal hope which is limited to the future well-being of the earthly city.

* * *

It is of the essence of hope [1] to hold a positive attitude in regard to time. This attitude which seems so reasonable to modern man, the ancients would have found very strange. Time to them was an enemy. A revolt against time, Mircea Eliade tells us, was characteristic of primitive religions. Rites were performed to abolish time by imitating archetypes. Whatever was without an exemplar was without meaning. There was never anything new in the world. Disregard for time was especially marked in ancient India. Time consisted of a series of rebirths which in their turn brought about new beginnings. It was the part of a wise man to free himself from these rebirths, by rejoining the eternal part of himself which was identical with the eternal principle of all things.

The same is true of thinkers in ancient Greece. Plato thought that the real world was the world of archetypal ideas and that the world of time was an illusion, a changing image of eternity. Aristotle believed that the individual existence and the single event were without meaning : only the

---

[1] Translator's note : Throughout this chapter Father DANIÉLOU has carefully distinguished between *esperance* (Christian hope) and *espoir* (temporal hope). From the context the English reader will be able to avoid any confusion of meaning.

unchanging laws regulating the universe were valid. Similarly in our own time Brunschwieg teaches that mathematical laws are the only true reality and reproaches Christians for attaching so much importance to personal existence. The Stoics conceived history to be an eternal return in which nothing could ever be new; and in recent years Nietzsche and Spengler have repeated this pagan vision.

Even where time is not condemned as evil, it is held to be suspect. The wise man expects nothing. That is the secret of happiness. To have no desires is the best way to have no disappointments. Never let fortune determine happiness. Such is the wisdom of Buddha : freedom from desires means freedom from suffering. Such was the wisdom of the Stoics : distinguish between what we can and cannot control, and attach ourselves only to the former. Such was the goal of a man like Gide : claiming the possession of Olympian wisdom and longing to die having lost all hope. Such also the goal of Camus, Malraux, Montherlant and so many other present day thinkers who affirm that it is man's greatness to have no other end, that to look for any reward is to vilify this greatness, and that a tragic end is to achieve the plenitude of greatness.

All this is another way of saying that the Bible completely reversed all values when it gave meaning to time and placed hope in the future. The man who knows the Bible thinks of time as the place where a divine plan is being shaped and he looks forward to the completion of this plan.

Hope is, for him, this looking forward. Thus he avoids what seemed natural to the pagans — a nostalgia for the past. Jean Héring writes that " The Christian ideal is not the exiled princess longing to return, it is Abraham setting out towards an unknown land which God will show him. " Ulysses, the hero of the ancients, after his years of wandering returns to his starting point and thus cancels time. Abraham knew no return. He left Ur of the Chaldees and never went back. He embarked on " the adventure of time, " forgetting, as Saint Paul tells us, " what was behind so as to stretch forward to things that are ahead. "

Faith in the future was from the first the special message of the Bible. Hope, henceforth, was to move like some refreshing breeze through the pessimism of the ancient world. But with the passage of the years it lost its religious roots and became secularized. In the seventeenth century Voltaire dared to substitute faith in progress for Bossuet's faith in providence. In the nineteenth century, prodigious technical advances made man set no limits to his own powers. This new faith hastened the spread of capitalism. As this declines, communism strives to take its place. Even now these two forms of optimism confront us : western liberalism as presented by Jaspers and Toynbee, or eastern communism as presented by the Marxists.

Rightly do Christians denounce modern optimism and declare that it has nothing in common with the theological virtue of hope. Great Christian thinkers of the last years of the nineteenth century and the early years of the twentieth, a Bloy, a Péguy, a Papini, a Chesterton cannot find words sufficiently sarcastic to deride the myth of progress. No one can deny that their attitude is in many ways justified. Faith in progress is a caricature of hope. Resting, as it does on man's power not God's, it is without any foundation or norm and it is doomed to misadventures. Limited to earthly perspectives, it has no place for hope in the future resurrection and life everlasting which are based on Christ's rising from the dead.

But if Christians of our day have been right in their denunciations of the illusions of the myth of progress, they have often fallen into a pessimism which regards the future with distrust and they have taken their stand with the forces of conservatism against the forces of progress. A salutary realism, which gives Christians a sense of sin and a spirit of detachment from what is human, ought not prevent Christians from sharing legitimate aspirations for the improvement of the conditions of human life.

Here we must pause to clarify our position. When we speak of human *hope*, we ought to distinguish between two differnt realities. Hope may be understood to mean an ideological optimism which is a secular degradation of the theological virtue of hope. A Christian can have no part in optimism of this kind. Or it may be considered as an aspiration towards better living conditions; many men are filled with this desire, either, because of the sub-human level of life around them, or because they have been led to believe that modern technical advances promise such improvement. Christians may well share these aspirations.

Therefore it is our right, in fact it is our duty, to share the temporal hopes of the men of our era. This is an era of hope. We are not always aware of this because we are not always filled with hope : only the poor hope, we are often rich. . . . But we ought to open ourselves to hope, even if we have many possessions. When I speak of the poor, I mean all who cannot find satisfaction for their legitimate aspirations for bread, work or freedom. Christians are obliged by their religion to take all suitable measures to further these aspirations. It is of the essence of Christianity to offer spiritual hope to all men, and it is now clear that Christianity also brings temporal hope to the poor of this world.

Moreover, modern men armed with all the new technical skills feel entitled to hope for great things. They are acquiring mastery over the material world and can make it serve them. They are gaining control over the biological world and can lessen pain and conquer disease. We know that the value of these advances depends on the use that is made of them, and that, alone, they are powerless to transform man. But we also think that they are good in themselves and that when men use them life becomes more human. Now this is precisely the Christian's duty. Technical progress is a fact. We need not deplore its dangers but we must take care that it contributes to man's true good. While some men face the future with anguish and see only what threatens them, we Christians must find reason for hope and set about building the new city.

* * *

Are these earthly hopes connected in any way with the theological virtue of hope? The answer, at first, seems to be no. The theological virtue is a firm assurance, based on God's fidelity to His promises, that we will obtain spiritual good things in this world and eternal life in the next. Is not its object God Himself? And is not its purpose to lift our desires above life here, where they rest?

And does not the Bible teach us from the first page to the last that God never promised earthly blessings to those who serve Him? Does not the book of Job warn us against such illusions? Is this not the answer to the apparent scandal of the injustice of a world in which the innocent so often suffer while their oppressors prosper? Is this not meant to teach us the true measure of earthly goods? Pius XI has written : " It is easy to see how little God thinks of riches because He gives them as often to His enemies as to His friends. "

Furthermore, did Christ ever promise earthly goods to His followers? True, He gave bread to hungry crowds, but He did this to teach them that there is another bread that comes down from heaven, and it was this bread He promised to send. Far from assuring His friends enjoyment here below, He announced that they would be persecuted for His name's sake. That is why Teresa of Avila cried out in the midst of her trials, " Lord, it is not surprising that you have so few friends. " But is there still room for temporal hope? Is this not enough to justify those who reproach Christians for dissuading souls from temporal tasks and urging them towards eternal goods?

In the political order we reach similar conclusions. If fidelity to God was the reason for some of the great victories of the past, national prosperity would be a proof of God's blessing, defeat a punishment. This is the claim of certain historians. Eusebius believed that Constantine's empire was the fulfillment of messianic prophecies, Bossuet found justification for monarchy in the kingship of Louis XIV. Nothing could be more dangerous than a theory of providence that sees success as a seal of divine approval. With far deeper insight Herbert Butterfield has pointed out that in the Old Testament the Chosen People could be unhappy and that the victory of pagan nations was not a sign of their election. The judgement of history is not the judgement of God. Hope is the expectancy of those who await a judgement from God that is more just than that of history.

But this does not mean that in history there are no judgements of God. It is difficult to reconcile this with the mystery of the cross, yet this mystery does not destroy the primordial relation of justice and happiness. This seems to be a permanent search of the human heart. The cross, a temporal reverse, prevents this search from being satisfied on earth. It forces men to rise higher. It points to everlasting life. But it succeeds in negating the search on the earthly plane only by supposing its existence. Even though God does not always hear our prayers for temporal goods,

He still wants us to ask for such things. A mother's prayer, entrusting the life of her children to God, proceeds from a very sure intuition of a religious soul.

There is still another way in which human hopes are connected with the theological virtue. This is the bond that exists between the virtue of hope and charity. Let me explain what I mean. The theological virtue of hope is the expectation of eternal blessings. But the practice of charity is the condition Christ laid down for their possession. Now, we have said, that one of the objects of charity is to fulfill the aspirations of the poor. So the struggle in the earthly city to give bread to the hungry, to clothe the naked, is a prerequisite to becoming a citizen of the heavenly city. Christ Himself has said so. That is why he who gave drink to the thirsty, who sheltered the homeless, who visited the prisoners will be brought on the last day by the Judge into the Kingdom whose doors He alone can open. This is theological hope: the desire to possess eternal goods and the practice of charity alone makes this possible. This same practice of charity is also the surest guarantee of civilization and the safest foundation for the temporal hopes of men.

In our day charity has acquired an institutional character. Individuals have only limited opportunities for doing good. Modern man knows that his greatest responsibility consists in improving institutions. In the depths of his conscience he knows that he will have to give the Sovereign Judge an account not only of his personal conduct but of the efforts he has made to solve wage and housing problems, and to promote world peace. He knows that a few private acts of charity will be no dispensation.

We have reached the heart of our problem. If all that we have said is true, Christians should now be the most active workers in the fight for social justice and international peace. Many today, even some non-Christians, see that Christianity is the only force capable of giving meaning to civilization. We agree yet we cannot hide the fact that for more than a century, despite certain brilliant achievements, Christianity has failed to meet this obligation. It has failed because many Christians, ignoring the repeated teaching of the Sovereign Pontiffs, have been motivated by an egoistic anxiety for their own personal salvation and by an exclusively self-interested concern about things temporal. These Christians have forgotten the bond that links these two activities. They have disregarded their absolute obligation to further the reign of God's law, which is justice and charity. First, they must be converted to this law; else they can never influence civilization.

The collapse we are witnessing today is not that of the social doctrine of the Church because this doctrine has been but laxly applied. The collapse is that of a Christian world not truly Christian. Yet the world is turning even now to Christianity. It is not the world that doubts Christians, but Christians who no longer believe in themselves. They do not believe in the social efficacy of their faith. Their disbelief springs from a bad conscience. Lastly, their disbelief is a form of laziness and a kind of comfort that dispenses them from effort. They settle down with pleasant hopes about the hereafter and they dispense themselves from working for the betterment of man's temporal condition. But things are not quite that simple. It is in struggling for the present city that the future city is won.

* * *

It is plain that human hopes are not unrelated to the virtue of hope, and that they are diametrically opposed to the atheistic optimism of the modern world. This is what we must now show. Atheistic optimism is based exclusively on man and on the mythical powers with which it endows him. While Christian hope is a theological virtue because it depends on God and on the promises that He has made to Abraham and which have been substantially fulfilled in Jesus Christ. Nor can we fail to add that hope is, in a sense, present wherever there is prayer, that is to say wherever a man, conscious of his powerlessness, appeals to God. Where there is religion there will always be prayer.

Modern man is tempted to hope in himself. Surrounded by all the power now under his control, man today believes he can save himself. He resents dependence of any kind. Because he is able to transform the conditions of life, he thinks he is able to transform himself and make himself the *demiurge* of the future. He trusts his own strength. He finds recourse to God repugnant.

Besides, he sees God as an obstacle to his development. He thinks that he achieves his full stature only when he is his own highest value, and that humanism is only real when it denies God. Man believes he is self-sufficient. Modern man's temptation is to want to show that he can do good without God, and that he can succeed where the lowly Gospel has failed.

We must denounce this false optimism which is a secularized and negated hope. We must denounce it, first, because it denies eternal salvation, the supreme object of hope. We must denounce it, also, because it is false even in the temporal domain. It supposes a belief that the intrinsic efficacy of progress, the strength of technology, the improvement of society can create a better mankind. We have already said that we believe in the value of human progress. But we also think that it is perfectly ambiguous.

Experience has shown only too clearly that economic laws left to themselves do not bring about a just distribution of wealth and that the scientific organization of society alone does not assure the full enjoyment of liberty. The worst enemy of true human progress is the myth of a false optimism which leads men to believe that it is enough to change the conditions of material existence, to transform the state of mankind. Now this is false under every aspect. Economic and technical progress are ambivalent and can put man into servitude as easily as they can free him. Even when employed in the best possible way, all they can do is to create more favorable conditions for man but they can never solve his problems. Man knows that he can receive answers to his ultimate problems only from the immolated Lamb who alone is able to open the sealed book in which is inscribed the destiny of all mankind.

But does not Christianity's refusal to trust blindly in man encourage him to neglect all temporal effort. The answer must be no. By a singular reversal Christianity exacts greater efforts from man because it knows his corrupt nature. It leads to indifference. Christianity knows what is in man's heart and that he is able to misuse the best things. It knows the obstacles that rise up in men's hearts against social justice, popular liberty, national union. It sees clearly. It can face the temptation even of despair because it knows it can conquer.

Peace and justice will not be ours without a struggle. They will not arrive as the result of a necessary evolution. They will not appear as the automatic result of certain economic transformations. They will exist if we *will* them and fight for them in an ever-renewed struggle. So many things are opposed to them. But true charity is stopped by no difficulty. According to the beautiful word of Paul : " Charity hopes for all things. " It is the inner force of a realistic act wisely directed to its end. It should not allow itself to be discouraged by anything. It has a special aptitude for meeting disasters without being disheartened. And it is its steadfastness that eventually vanquishes its adversaries.

It is, therefore, an illusion to believe that the myth of an earthly paradise in which man is a *demiurge* is necessary to stimulate action in time. Christians, whose hope is not of this world, must draw, from a charity that is to be practiced in the world, the strength to make the world better. They ought not suspect the future but take possession of it. We think they should give the searching world the soul it lacks. We think that the men of today, in the present crisis, need a temporal order that they can love and which is worthy of their sacrifices. We think that unless we offer them this temporal order, like disappointed lovers they will search elsewhere for another that is unworthy of what they have to give.

* * *

This human order must be bathed in divine grace and so it must not only be built by human hands but it must also come down from above, for " all best gifts descend from the Father of Light. " We think that if man expects this order to come from God only, he is lazy; but if he expects it to come only from himself, he is proud. This is the subtle problem of prayer and action. This is the mysterious secret of that little hope which Péguy calls the younger sister of the theological virtue. The effort that builds the city of man cannot be separated from the effort that builds the city of God.

Poverty

8

Without poverty, charity and truth there can be no spirit of the Gospel. And without the spirit of the Gospel there can be no Christian life. To be unfaithful to this spirit is to betray the essence of the Gospel. There are Christians today who fear they sin gravely against poverty. Those who have more than they need ask whether the possession of riches is compatible with the Gospel and they wonder what sacrifices they should make. Those who are poor but who are beginning to improve their financial position sometimes unselfishly question how far they are entitled to rise above their less privileged brothers. [1]

It is difficult to decide exactly what evangelical poverty entails. Does it demand a simple way of life and the suppression of all superfluities?

[1] This is especially true of French *Militants*. See " Les béatitudes dans la vie d'un militant ouvrier ", *Masses Ouvrières*, Nov. 1955, pp. 42-43.

Does it exact complete detachment and the possession of all things in common? Does it ask a more radical rupture and a complete dedication to the workman's struggle? Or, on the contrary, is it a purely interior attitude which can be easily reconciled with luxury and comfort? All these solutions have been suggested. In fact, here and there they have been tried. Yet they fail to satisfy.

This leads to the paradoxical claim that poverty is an integral part of the Gospel teaching and that it is difficult to discover how to practice it. So it is necessary that an attempt be made to throw some light on a question which is as obscure as it is vital. This is what we want to do here. First we must clarify the ambiguities of the term poverty; even in the Gospel its meanings vary; then we must show that the exaltation of poverty as an aspect of the Christian's royal dignity is not to be confused with the duty of charity that brings the Christian to the poor man in order to lift him from his poverty. Next we must ask what is essential to evangelical poverty. And in conclusion we will apply what we have discovered to some practical problems.

* * *

When we ask ourselves what Christ meant when He beatified the poor, two extreme solutions come at once to mind. The first answer stresses the last two words in the phrase " the poor in spirit. " This is equivalent to saying that evangelical poverty is above all an interior attitude of detachment in regard to material goods and that this attitude is perfectly compatible with the possession of these same goods. This solution, true though it be to a large degree, nevertheless seems too easy. It quickly expresses itself in a number of pharisaical positions because it is difficult to enjoy the good things of this world with a peaceful conscience when other men are in want. Here we touch an area where abuses are tolerated because of " a right intention. "

It must be admitted that the Gospel itself makes it difficult to accept this purely interior interpretation. In fact it is soon apparent, at least in Saint Luke, that the problem of riches is there understood in the strict sense. To the blessing promised to the poor there is a corresponding curse for the rich. So from the outset an overly simplified solution seems to us impossible. Poverty freed from costly privations would not be poverty. But it would be as great an error to claim that the privation of material goods is in itself an absolute and supreme value. In some places today this deviation is fairly common. That is why we shall insist on it first.

It is well to recall the distinction that Péguy makes between wretchedness and poverty. A first mistake would identify " the poor " of the beatitude with " the wretched. " By " the poor " or " the wretched " we here mean those who have the necessary minimum to realize a truly human life. Certainly these poor people hold an important place in the Christian perspective. It is of the essence of Christianity to go out to the lost and abandoned. To do this is to do what Christ did. His equality with God did not seem to Him to be something He should prize and He took the form of a slave. In a certain sense the Christian's place is with the poor and the disinherited of this world. He goes to them to draw them out of their wretchedness. This implies no exaltation of wretchedness nor even complicity with it. Mounier has stated quite correctly that, " In the Christian tradition there is no false cult of poverty or pain. "[1]

There are those who exalt the state of extreme poverty. Their position is ambiguous. It springs from a morbid complicity with degradation and is diametrically opposed to the Christian attitude. Christ held misery in horror just as He held in horror sickness and death. Nothing falsifies Him more than to attribute to Him complicity with the forces of destruction. He descends into wretchedness to rescue man but not man's wretchedness. An exaltation of wretchedness would be the expression of a *ressentiment* of values, this was the charge Nietzsche leveled against Christianity, and it is a pure perversion of the Gospel.

But there is a more moderate cult of poverty. A controversy that arose in the last congress of the C.G.T. (Centrale Générale du Travail) enabled French economists to refute the Communist claim that workers in capitalist countries are completely impoverished. Increased production and the action of social laws tend to raise living standards. Might this not lessen the worker's fighting spirit? Can there be a revolution without

[1] *De la propriété capitaliste à la propriété humaine*, p. 88.

a wretched and impoverished proletariat? Is it not possible that a decrease in the number of the poor might strengthen the power of the capitalists? We have heard Christians anxiously discussing these questions. Needless to say, even if such politically reprehensible tactics were employed, they would have nothing of the spirit of the Gospel about them. The poverty of the Gospels is not meant to hasten any revolution in the class struggle. [1]

This leads to our second idea about the poor in the Gospel. It, too, is sociological. It, too, claims that they are not the wretched ones, the proletariat, but the people, the great mass of country and city workers. Reference is always made to the fact that Christ was a worker; a remark that calls for certain distinctions. The text, " I have come to preach the Gospel to the poor, " is interpreted in terms applicable to the working class.

It is suggested that there is a kind of affinity between the Church and the people, and an incompatibility between Christ and the middle class.

In reply we might say that confusions of this kind have appeared throughout the history of Christianity. So it is useful to recall that Christianity is not the apanage of the middle class anymore than it is of the working class. To be a Christian it is not necessary to become a worker. To belong to the middle class is not an original sin. If the natural virtues of the working class : generosity, solidarity and simplicity are a fine preparation for the Gospel, this does not make

[1] Jean MASSIN makes this claim in *Le Festin chez Lévi*, p. 161.

them Gospel virtues. And it is dangerous to identify the Gospel with them. The middle class also possesses virtues which are not found in the Gospel, but which are an excellent preparation for the Gospel.

This position which does not exalt poverty but which does exalt the worker leads to a false attitude towards evangelical poverty. It renders suspect any improvement in standards of living or arouses fear of any increase in the number of the bourgeoisie. This is plain from a statement made by a militant Christian worker that I quoted in *Masses ouvrières* : " Poverty is the great question that confronts *militants*. They seek a more human, a more materially comfortable life for their household. This is normal under modern conditions. But the anxiety persists. " Mounier quite rightly condemned the confused thought that is at the root of this anxiety. Evangelical poverty does not consist in what he called " living the life of the poor. " [1] On the contrary it consists in working to raise the general standards of living. It is incorrect to equate poverty with the median level of working class life. A *militant* observed : " Poverty is not a trick that makes it possible to stay in the working class, nor is it an end in itself. " [2] This is the very formula that Saint Thomas used : " Poverty is not a good in itself. " [3]

In the worker's mind, poverty is connected with the standard of living. In the

---

[1] *Loc. cit.*, p. 89.
[2] *Loc. cit.*, p. 43. [3] *Contra Gentiles*, III, 134.

collectivist's mind poverty is connected with property. The first is on the level of use, the second of possession. The two are not necessarily related. In fact they may even be separated. A man may own great wealth and live frugally, either because of his avarice or his ideals. Admirable examples abound of men of vast fortunes who lived in poverty and gave their wealth to others. Reciprocally within a community where property is not possessed individually (either a religious order or a collectivist society) the use of goods may vary.

Confusion will follow if evangelical poverty is identified with goods held in common. Passages in the Acts of the Apostles will be recalled where it is said that the first Christians held all in common. Under these conditions an act of proprietorship would be considered incompatible with the spirit of the Gospel. The conclusion might be drawn that all societies founded on private property are intrinsically evil and scandal could be taken because the Church has never condemned them categorically. This could be considered as infidelity to the Gospel. Reciprocally a basic affinity might be affirmed between Christianity and communism, and some might wonder why the Church condemned this system, not only because of its metaphysical propositions, but also because of its rejection of the right of private property.

Clearly the question is complex. It cannot be denied that communal ownership was practised in primitive communities and is still practised in religious communities, where communal possession is the object of the vow of poverty.

Therefore, although there is a connection between holding all things in common and evangelical poverty, it would be erroneous to make this an end, since it is only a means, and to find the essence of evangelical poverty in communal ownership, or to assume that the former cannot exist where the latter is absent.

The example of the first Christian community has no probative value in this instance. In fact, far from being something specifically Christian, the common ownership of goods, on the contrary, appears to be one of the elements that was most certainly borrowed from outside. Manuscripts discovered near the Dead Sea show that this custom was fairly prevalent among fervent Jews in those days. It is to be found in other religions, as well. It appears in Christianity as a means of perfection but not as a constitutive element.

This is all the more evident if common ownership of goods is considered sociologically. To equate collectivism and Christianity purely and simply on the basis of property is crass confusion. In reality, communal and personal holdings are two poles which are equally necessary to economic life and both must be safeguarded. The Constitution of the Year 89 was right when it made the right of private ownership one of the rights of the human person and defended it as a legitimate liberty; it was wrong when it gave an incomplete and partly false idea of this right. Socialism quite correctly recalled, on the other hand, that the community had a certain claim on productive goods and refused to allow a few individuals to possess what was intended for the use of all. Therefore the Church has always stressed both aspects. But this has nothing to do with evangelical poverty.

** *

So far we have tried to free evangelical poverty from some confused ideas that hid its real meaning. It seems to us that it cannot be identified with any specific form of effective poverty, while at the same time it is not a purely interior disposition lacking any external expression. Now we must face the question positively and ask ourselves in what it does consist. To explain it with merely human perspectives would be to err. To understand it, we must go back to Scripture and find out what its pages teach about the word " poor. " There we learn that this word like so many others (justice for example) has a meaning in the Bible that is different from that of daily use. It is to be expected that Christians will make mistakes unless we can give them the right meaning.

Here, as almost always, if we are to understand the New Testament we must begin with the Old. In many places, especially in the psalms, reference is made to the poor, the *anawim*. But the description we find there may at first surprise us.

The poor man seems to be someone who is oppressed. He is persecuted by the powerful. He suffers from their calumnies, he is stripped of his goods, he is trapped by misfortune. Material privation is only one of his many trials. In itself this state is nowhere considered to be a value. On the contrary the poor man longs for deliverance. But this he expects from God alone. He is perfectly sure that some day God will come and save him.

Occasionally these texts are interpreted as indicative of the social conflicts that divided the people of Israel. Prophets and psalmists, it is alleged, expressed the protests of the common people against the exorbitant demands of the powerful, the wealthy landowners or high dignitaries. It is true that some of the texts do refer to the poor in sociological terms : " The psalmists describe the oppression of those who were the victims of social injustice, or who suffered from vexations imposed by the insolent rich or a domineering judge. " [1] But nothing could be further from the truth than to think of the prophets and psalmists as champions in the class struggle, men who sought to free the proletariat from the exploitation of the rich. Andrew Neher has made it admirably clear that this was not part of their outlook. [2]

So we see that this aspect of oppression is only secondary. In the Bible the poor are above all " the pious, " " the just. " These are the men who are faithful to God's law. Their fidelity is a basic part of this concept. Poverty is defined essentially in its relation to God and not first of all in relation to material goods or to other men. This alone makes biblical poverty unique. It belongs to a world of thought in which the relation to

[1] A. GELIN, *Les pauvres de Jahweh*, p. 54.
[2] *Amos*, p. 136; cf. Chapter III, Obedience.

God is primary and dominates everything else. The poor man is the man who keeps God's law. He suffers because this law is not observed by all men. He hungers and thirsts for justice; this phrase, too, must be understood in the biblical sense, where it means the accomplishment of God's will.

The poor man inevitably comes in conflict with the powerful ones of this world. These "rich" men are not the possessors of material goods, nor do they sit in high places, but they are the men who, instead of obeying God's law at the expense of their own interests, serve their own interests at the expense of God's law. Conflict is inevitable. The "poor" are a living reproach to the "rich." Their struggle to establish God's law forces them to struggle against man's ingrained selfishness. This makes them the object of sarcasm, mistreatment, persecution. Poverty leads us into the heart of the Bible, to the center of the battle between the two cities which makes up its warp and woof.

The importance of all this to an understanding of biblical poverty is obvious. First, it is clear that poverty is not to be defined in any kind of sociological context but in relationship to God. The poor man is one who gives priority to God's will because he has understood that God is to be preferred above all else. Our frame of reference is religious and is that of the whole Bible. But at the same time fidelity to God leads inevitably to material consequences. Anyone who takes God seriously cannot fail to compromise his reputation, sacrifice his interests, lose his tranquillity. True poverty cannot be "poverty in miniature." It can never soothe the conscience and make possible a carefree life. To practise evangelical poverty is to accept great risks and requires unfailing fidelity to God's law. There is no need to go in search of poverty. It will come unbidden — it will come sooner than it is expected. Those who take God seriously are sure to be poor. This is the concept of poverty that we find in the Old Testament. We find the same concept in the New Testament. In a study of the beatitudes made recently by Jacques Dupont, he observes that their essence seems to be expressed in Christ's first and last blessings, that is to say in the one that refers to poverty and the one that refers to persecution. [1] This is a splendid confirmation of what we noticed in the Old Testament. The poor are necessarily the persecuted. Conversely, Christians who are well treated by the world should find this disturbing. They should ask themselves if they have purchased this kindness with their compromises.

Somewhere else Dom Dupont has written that these two beatitudes provide us with a key to all the others. All eight may be traced back to one attitude. Whether it be a question of "justice," or "kingdom," or "earth," in every case, there is a thirst to accomplish God's will, not only on the personal plane but also on the collective plane. This must be fulfilled, first of all, on the spiritual plane, and this means the realization of God's plan which is the growth

[1] *Les Béatitudes*, pp. 15-26.

of the Mystical Body, and also on the temporal plane where fidelity to God exacts that respect be paid to the laws that regulate human society. Therefore the poor man will be led to combat social injustice, not because of class solidarity but because of obedience to God.

This attitude (the New Testament here repeats what we found in the Old) necessarily forces the poor man to compromise his own interests. " You cannot serve God and Mammon, " Christ says. To follow God seriously, perforce means to lose the world's point of view. One cannot seek at the same time personal success and the success of God's work : " He who would save his life must lose it and he who loses it because of Me will save it. " A follower of Christ must be a man who has lost reputation, repose, fortune. [1] The servant cannot be greater than the Master. Christ was the first to wish to lose all. He is the Poor Man. His follower must be poor, too.

These scriptural facts change the perspective in which we look at poverty. They substitute the single rule of God's will for all personal ends because men can become attached to poverty, if it is made an end in itself. Pascal used to say that it is possible to turn truth into an idol. In the same way we may make an idol out of poverty. And it is precisely here that we find the source of the errors that we mentioned at the beginning of this chapter : the identification of poverty with a certain standard of life, a certain sociological plane, a certain distribution of wealth.

[1] See *The Lord of History*, passim.

But evangelical poverty is free, even in regard to poverty. It is free in every respect except in regard to the will of God. Privation is good when it is willed by God, but prosperity would be good, too, when it is willed by God. To attach one's self to privation would be to attribute too great an importance to earthly goods. Christ formulated the evangelical law when He said : " Be not concerned about what you eat or what you drink, nor wherewith you will be clothed. Seek first the kingdom of God and His justice. " But that may also mean : " Do not be concerned about what you do not eat, or do not drink, or wherewith you do not clothe yourself. " Non-use is no more perfect than use. But use is good if it is willed by God, and non-use is good if it is willed by God.

This was Christ's way during much of His life. It has often been pointed out that He was not an ascetic like John the Baptist. He, Himself said to the Jews : " For John came neither eating nor drinking, and they say, ' He has a devil! ' The Son of Man came eating and drinking, and they say, ' Behold a glutton and a wine-drinker ... ' " (Matt. 11 : 18-19). Christ led common life. He made no diet mandatory. He practised no ascetic singularities. He saw the good things of this world as His Father's gift. He used them with gratitude. But He also knew how to do without them when this was His Father's will. He was thirsty when He waited at the Samaritan well. He had no stone on which to rest His head.

This is evangelical poverty. It does not consist in following an attraction for privation as if this were a good in itself but it does consist in accepting privation, if God asks this. Saint Paul expresses this in a lapidary phrase : " I am able to abound and I am able to be indigent. " That is to say, that neither indigence nor abundance matter. What does matter is the kingdom of God and His justice. And this " in honor and dishonor, in evil report and good report; as deceivers and yet truthful, as unknown and yet well known, as dying and behold, we live, as chastised but not killed, as sorrowful yet always rejoicing, as poor yet enriching many, as having nothing yet possessing all things " (2 Cor. 6 : 8-10).

Thus we see that evangelical poverty is the disposition of a soul uniquely concerned about the interests of the kingdom of God and free in regard to earthly goods. It is the expression of the dignity of the Son of God. When we are invited to take part in the Banquet with the sons, it is undignified to delay over the crumbs under the table, they are for the little dogs. Not that crumbs are to be despised. But what matters is : " Seek thy glory where it is to be found, " as Saint John of the Cross says, " do not waste time over the crumbs that fall from your Father's table. Thus you will find your heart's desire. " We sin against evangelical poverty when attachment to our own comfort, to our reputation, or to our interests, prevent us from fulfilling a known and explicit will of God. Preoccupation is a sin against poverty. " Be troubled about nothing, " says Saint Paul. Tauler speaks of Christ " living free from all preoccupation and receiving all things moment by moment from His Father. "

We have tried to show what is original in evangelical poverty. We have seen that it refers essentially to God, as do the Christian dispositions of charity, obedience, humility. As a function of the primacy of God and His kingdom, it is seen to be a judgement and a line of action in regard to earthly goods. The primacy of God demands a basic liberty in regard to all created things, not that they should be disparaged or rejected, but that their use should always be regulated according to the demands of the divine will. As a matter of fact these demands will always lead to sacrifice. They will turn the Christian into a lost man, lost to himself, lost to the world, freed from the world and from himself, that is to say it will turn him into a free man.

But this basic disposition must be realized in concrete fashion. We have shown that evangelical poverty is to be identified neither with poverty, nor a simple way of life, nor with collectivism and the sharing of all goods. Yet these different forms of actual poverty, are not, for that reason, valueless. Although they are not to be identified with poverty, they may be used as means of the practising of poverty. And this is what we must now consider.

We have said that evangelical poverty consists in being free in regard to earthly goods, so that they may be used or not used. But concretely men do not enjoy this freedom, that is to say they are naturally attached to earthly goods. So that there is always the danger that the day God asks that they be sacrificed, man will find himself unprepared. Therefore, this liberty must be acquired. To acquire this liberty, we must go against our natural tendency to become attached to comfort, reputation, pleasures, money, ambition. The actual privation of these things becomes, therefore, an ascetical necessity. We have said that in itself this is not a value and is not to be sought for its own sake. This search is asceticism, as long as it is not a human technique, but it is not evangelical poverty. It is to be found in many places, among Indian monks, among Greek sages, among members of primitive religions. But the Christian will set about its practice as necessary training if he is to remain free.

Pleasures are not to be enjoyed, nor money handled without danger. The enjoyment of pleasures always stimulates our instincts; while this is not wrong in itself, there is also a psychological reaction. Development in every way at the same time is impossible. Gide was wrong when he claimed that man can develop both his sensuality and his spirituality at the same time. Saint Augustine expressed this admirably : " If you wish to widen the area of love, you must restrict the area of the flesh. " Actual poverty, frugality of diet, simplicity of life, create a favorable climate for spiritual life : " Nothing disposes us more favorably for prayer than to live on a handful of dates and clear water, " according to Psichari.

The same is true of riches. They are a source of innumerable temptations because of the opportunities they afford. They are also a source of preoccupations which leave little liberty to devote to the service of God. That is why, as we have seen, beside the beatitude that Matthew gives us which considers poverty solely as a spiritual attitude, Luke offers an interpretation that stresses the advantages of actual poverty and warns us against riches. The malediction pronounced against riches, is in no way, as we have said, a condemnation of riches as such but it is a warning that they are an obstacle to the practice of evangelical poverty. This is the net that Satan uses to capture the soul and carry it into his army.

So it is not wealth that is wicked. And it is God's will for some men to dispose of great fortunes. But it is we who are wicked. And because we are wicked, creatures are dangerous. It is not more perfect to be blind than to have two eyes. But it is better to be blind and enter the kingdom than not to enter it and keep two eyes. " If thy eye scandalize thee, pluck it out. " There may be cases where riches are so dangerous that it is a duty to renounce them in order to save one's soul. This explains the vocation of many monks. There is always the obligation of protecting one's self from the danger they offer and of practising certain effective renunciations, else they will become strong enough to destroy spiritual liberty and evangelical poverty.

The same is true of common ownership and the renunciation of property. We have said that evangelical poverty does not condemn the private appropriation of goods : this is a sociological reality and is based on man's nature. To own property is not a sin and is perfectly compatible with evangelical poverty. But this poses several problems. Ownership is inseparable from responsibility. Its problems are those of every form of temporal charge. They do not differ essentially in the head of a large firm, the important official, the big bondholder, the statesman.

Far from believing that there is any incompatibility between the responsibilities of these men and evangelical poverty, I hold on the contrary that it would be a profound illusion for them not to look for evangelical poverty in their responsibilities. This is what I mean. Some men think of evangelical poverty in a slightly imaginative and poetic way, " the duty of carelessness. " To them the spirit of the Gospel is a form of irresponsibility that comes from spiritual childishness. They divide their lives in two parts. There is their professional and social temporal life; this yields only anxiety. Then there is their private life redolent of the Gospel. Poverty is a cause for amusement. But this is to mock poverty.

Evangelical poverty is meant to reach the heart of our existence. It is no more opposed to the responsibilities connected with money, than with any others. A great Christian life is a life charged with responsibilities, overwhelmed with work. But poverty requires us to carry these responsibilities with great liberty of spirit and to do this work without any preoccupation. Evangelical poverty in this instance would not consist in renouncing property but in assuming it as a responsibility. In this way it is placed at the service of the common good. In fact property as an institution is not contrary to evangelical poverty but the spirit of appropriation, which uses material goods to gratify selfish pleasure and ambition, and refuses to accept the service it entails, is contrary to this virtue.

From this point of view evangelical poverty reveals itself as an aptitude for not keeping what one has for one's self but for sharing all things with others. This in no way involves the suppression of personal property but the destruction of avarice and of the spirit of possessiveness. It would be ideal if people would share what they have, or if the community were based on an exchange of gifts, or goods were considered as common not because private property was abolished but because of the free communication each one makes to others of what is his. This is the ideal of the Christian community and it is, as it were, a reflection of the community of the Three divine Persons where each Person gives Himself wholly to the others. Is not an application of this spirit to be found in the duty of hospitality and in the desire to reduce one's own extravagant expenditures in favor of the wretched?

Nevertheless a situation might arise in which evangelical poverty would require the holding of all goods in common and the renunciation of all property rights. But this occurs only in special cases and does not constitute its essence. Religious orders are an example of this. A renunciation of the right to hold property is justified by the fact that even when this is done in the spirit of poverty it still entails work with all the usual earthly cares. God frees some men from this responsibility so that they can consecrate themselves more completely to spiritual things and the service of God's kingdom. If the primacy of God's kingdom is an essential aspect of evangelical poverty, then this freedom from earthly cares is seen to be an eminent form of evangelical poverty. But it is only an eminent form.

We have not yet considered one of the aspects of poverty that we alluded to at the beginning of this chapter : this is suffering poverty. We said that this, like other forms of actual poverty, was not an essential part of evangelical poverty. But it does not follow that it is totally unrelated. Yet the reasons why men embrace it, are not practical reasons as in the two preceding cases. From the point of view of wisdom it is absolutely unjustifiable. It is folly. But to a Christian this folly seems sovereignly desirable, because it was first embraced by Christ.

Here we reach the mystery of the Cross. The Word of God coming into the world did not choose for Himself honors, riches, prosperity. Nor did He condemn them. But He did not select them for Himself. He elected opprobrium, humiliations, privations. He alone had the right to make this choice. No one can do this on his own initiative. Yet it is understandable that through the centuries Christ's friends have longed to share His lot, the better to resemble Him. So Francis of Assisi espoused Lady Poverty; Ignatius of Loyola asked in his *Spiritual Exercises* to imitate Christ by enduring all injury and contempt, all poverty actual as well as spiritual; so Pascal wrote : " I love poverty because He loved it; " so Père de Foucauld went to Nazareth in search of " the abjection " of Jesus. It is impossible to be a Christian unless one walks more or less boldly in this direction.

Certainly, as we have said, evangelical poverty may be practised in " good repute as well as in evil repute, " in " prosperity as well as in privation. " It is above all freedom in regard to the one and the other. The abjection of Jesus might in itself become an idol. The only right attitude is love of the divine will, holy indifference. But within this indifference, within this evangelical poverty, a preference is permitted. Christ's friends will always prefer poverty and abjection because such was the lot of their Master. Pure indifference could be the law in a sinless world. But in a world plunged in pleasure and permeated with ambition, in a world in thrall to honor and wealth, folly must match folly : the folly of the cross must redeem the folly of the world.

*
* *

In conclusion, let us answer the question we asked at the beginning of this study. Poverty is at the heart of the Christian existence. Christians have a right to experience it. But it would be an error to want to identify poverty with any of its forms. These forms are not foreign to it. But their value depends on a deeper, inner attitude. This attitude is Christianity itself, inasmuch as it is seriously concerned with the kingdom of God and His justice. Every attempt to understand poverty in any other perspective is to falsify its meaning. But in this perspective all other forms find their meaning. They are special realizations, according to special vocations, of the universal vocation of every Christian to be poor.

Printed in Belgium by DESCLÉE & Cie, ÉDITEURS, S. A. Tournai. — 10.404